One Nation Under God:
The Virtues That Made America

Jerry M. Roper, Ph.D.

BookLocker
Trenton, Georgia

Print ISBN: 978-1-958892-46-6
Ebook ISBN: 979-8-88531-711-5

Published by BookLocker.com, Inc., Trenton, Georgia.

BookLocker.com, Inc.
2024

First Edition

Library of Congress Cataloguing in Publication Data
Roper, Ph.D., Jerry M.
One Nation Under God: The Virtues That Made America by Jerry M. Roper, Ph.D.
Library of Congress Control Number: 2024907635

For Lisa, Emily, and Eric.

Acknowledgements

As 21st Century Americans, we are inheritors of a nation built by men and women, who believed that the American way of life and the nation's well-being was secured not by our wealth, our military might, or our form of representative government. Instead, they believed that the nation's motto "In God We Trust" represented the true guardian and guarantor of our liberty and the American way of life. Ensuing from this trust in God was a desire to build a moral and virtuous nation. These previous generations of virtuous and moral Americans are for the most part anonymous, every day, ordinary people, who made mistakes yet got so much right, as they made a nation under God. How can these Americans be adequately acknowledged for their contribution to this book? Historian and author, Stephen Ambrose, in his book, "Citizen Soldiers: The U.S. Army from the Normandy Beaches to the Bulge to the Surrender of Germany," captured the essence of virtuous Americans when he wrote the following: "At the core, the American citizen soldiers knew the difference between right and wrong, and they didn't want to live in a world in which wrong prevailed. So they fought, and won, and all of us, living and yet to be born, must be forever profoundly grateful."

Courage, wisdom, justice, resolve, perseverance, and gratitude, these are virtues that Ambrose identified as characterizing the average American soldier. The writing of this book in the 21st Century could not be possible without the virtue and sacrifice of the Greatest Generation in the 20th Century. Therefore, they are gratefully acknowledged by the author, who had the privilege of witnessing how they lived their lives. They provided the inspiration to attempt to convey to a new generation of Americans the virtue of the nation they have now inherited.

This project of identifying and telling how virtue shaped America could not and was not accomplished alone. My wonderful wife, Lisa, patiently listened to ideas, read drafts, and gave candid criticism when needed and genuine praise when merited. My daughter, Emily, and I collaborated on shorter pieces related to this book, and her skill as a writer and editor improved mine. Jan Packwood graciously edited and proofed the manuscript, and did much more. She believed in the project and shared the conviction that for America to endure a new generation of Americans must seek virtue.

Table of Contents

Author's note:

Open sources readily available through Web searches
provided general background information for each chapter.
Because these sources are readily accessible and to avoid
incumbering the reader with footnotes, general background
information sources are not cited. However, references are
provided for all quotes, and books relied upon are cited at the end
of chapters. Unless otherwise noted, all scriptural quotes are from
Zondervan's New International Version (NIV).

Reader! whoever thou art, remember this, and in thy Sphere, practice Virtue thyself, and encourage it in others.

The Last Will & Testament of Patrick Henry, 1799

Chapter 1.
VIRTUE... hidden and forgotten in today's America

What happened to virtue in America is entirely explained by an incident that occurred over a century ago at a world famous health spa. To tell this story, it's best to begin at the beginning. For approximately three thousand years, Bath, England has been known for the curative powers of its thermal springs. Bladud, the king of the ancient Britons is credited with discovering the springs around 860 B.C. According to legend, King Bladud developed a most unpleasant skin condition. Fearing it was leprosy, the Britons banished their king and he became a wandering pig herder. One day when passing through the Bath region, his pigs found a warm muddy hole, wallowed in it, and slept in it overnight. The next morning, Bladud, who seemingly was meticulous about his pigs, washed the mud off. To his astonishment, their hides were smooth, and their skin as pink and healthy as that of a newborn piglet. He reasoned if it worked for pigs, it could work for him. He bathed in the mud and his skin healed. Bladud returned to the Britons, his crown was restored, and word of the healing power of the hot mineral waters at Bath spread. But, the story doesn't end here.

Eight hundred years later in 60 A.D., the Romans decided to take the hot springs to a whole new level. They built an impressive temple to Sulis Minerva, a local deity that was created by merging a Celtic god, Sulis, with the Roman god, Minerva. The temple complex included a pool filled with water from the hot mineral springs. Bath now had a proper spa! By the 5th Century, the Romans were gone from Britain, and over the ensuing centuries, the City of Bath developed. In the 12th Century, a new bath was built over the site used by the Romans,

1

and in fact, the new bath used the old Roman walls and columns to support the new pool's foundation. A statue of King Bladud was commissioned and placed so that it overlooked the new bath, and from the statue came the name, the King's Bath.

From the 12th to the 20th Century, the King's Bath remained in use, and over the centuries the area around it developed with several significant structures being added such as commercial buildings, apartments, and shops. These buildings followed the example of the King's Bath, and used the Roman foundations to support the new construction. Over the centuries the magnificent bath, spa, and temple complex built by the Romans disappeared beneath the growing City of Bath.

In the 18th Century, the famous Grand Pump Room, which remains in use, was built adjacent to the King's Bath. In 1873, however, a problem developed. The King's Bath sprang a leak and Major Charles Davis, the City of Bath's surveyor and architect, set about to discover its origin and fix it. His search took him deep under the pool and into the old Roman foundation. There he found corridors and adjoining rooms with ornate tile floors. He continued exploring farther and farther until he was well away from the King's Bath foundation. He was now in subbasements of nearby buildings.

In the dim torch light, he could see that he was standing in a large open space, and as he felt his way around, he discovered stone columns and handsome statuary. All of it was from the Roman period, and all of it was hidden in the subbasements of buildings. Decade by decade, as buildings came and went, got larger and more complex the original Roman bath and temple complex disappeared from view and vanished from memory. Thankfully, the Roman craftsmanship was so substantial that it endured over the centuries and supported the modern City of Bath, whose citizens were unaware of the incredible beauty, timeless significance, and ancient value that lay beneath their feet. And, so it is with the virtues.

Virtues, and in particular Christian virtues, are the foundation of Western civilization. They are ancient. Their value and significance cannot be overstated. Virtues afford incredible beauty to the lives of all who practice them, and the society that honors, respects, and teaches virtue to each generation is a society that flourishes. But, just as the stunning Roman temple and bath lay hidden and forgotten in a subbasement, so also have America's virtues. In our rush into 21st Century modernism, we are like the medieval builders. America has overlaid our foundation of sturdy virtues with an insubstantial slab made of high sounding principles, seemingly noble but empty values, and a watery feel good Christianity where Jesus is not Lord of all, but just a good buddy. Like plastic, these modern feel good notions are flimsy and unsuitable foundational material to support a thriving civilization.

Over the decades, America's new faux and virtueless foundation has held up more or less well. However, we are now realizing that high sounding principles, empty values, and a watered down Christianity are nothing more than vapid platitudes. Lacking virtue and God, we have nothing to restrain evil and promote good. In this continuing state of moral decline, our iniquities have been piling higher and higher to the point that we are running out of sins to commit. Therefore, we have set our depraved minds to dreaming up new ways to sin, and our flimsy virtueless foundation can no longer bear the weight of such immorality. The faux foundation of our society is cracking. We have sprung a multitude of leaks, and more are on the way.

Our way out of this dilemma is to be like Major Charles Davis. We must go deep into America's subbasement. Just as Major Davis discovered the enduring beauty of the Roman temple and bath, we will discover the splendor and beauty of ancient and timeless virtues that have been buried and hidden beneath our feet. The virtues have not gone away. They're all still there waiting for us. Each of the following chapters highlights a virtue and tells the story of how that virtue made America. When all the virtues are explained and all the stories are told, we will be like Major Davis on that day in 1873. We will be astonished by the ancient and enduring quality and beauty of America's real foundation, and we will be equally incredulous that something of such importance could have ever been hidden, forgotten, and lost. Now, let's get going! Light your torches! We are going deep into our nation's true foundation, where we will discover the virtues that made America.

Chapter 2.
HUMILITY... the soil in
which virtue blooms

"Blessed are the meek, for they will inherit the earth." (Matthew 5:5)

Do we, 21st Century Americans, believe this statement? Jesus said it. It's the third "Blessed" statement in Jesus' Sermon on the Mount, which even non-Christians recognize as the most profound of all moral teachings. Therefore, it must be true, but do we believe it? Meek, according to the Merriam-Webster dictionary, is synonymous with humble, modest, and timid. Related descriptive words are mousy, unassertive, and cowering. American parents never raise their children to have any of these characteristics. In fact, we train our children to grow into adults who are outgoing, assertive, and bossy, because that's how you get ahead in this world. "Lead, follow, or get out of the way!" That's the American way. Meekness and humility have been all but driven out of the American culture, and to what effect? What kind of earth – the land, the nation, the society – will our children inherit? Previous generations of Americans inherited this land of Washington, Jefferson, and Lincoln; a land with a national holiday devoted to humbly giving thanks to God; a land with "In God We Trust" stamped on its currency; a land of freedom and hope; a land that President Reagan said is "a shining city upon a hill." This too is derived from Jesus' Sermon on the Mount. *Ye are the light of the world. A city that is set on an hill cannot be hid.* (Matthew 5:14 KJV)

Could it be that our children's inheritance depends upon humility, and that the meek – not the proud, arrogant, and bossy - will inherit the land just as Jesus said? To answer this question, we're going to board a ship docked in the harbor on the Isle of

Wight. The name of the ship is the *Arabella,* and the year is 1630. The *Arabella* has a timeless story to tell, because at its core is a story of humility, whose Latin root is *humus* (earth). From the men and women on this voyage, we will learn that the substance – the *humus* – of our souls is what shapes the society in which we live and bequeath to our children. But, we need to make haste. The *Arabella* is departing and we must be on it.

* * *

Aboard the *Arabella*, Isle of Wight, April 1630.

The air is crisp and clear, and on our cheeks we feel a gentle south breeze. The north winds of March are in retreat, and once the sails are hoisted, the captain says we'll quickly be on our way to America. This voyage has been organized by the Massachusetts Bay Company under the leadership of a landed gentleman and lawyer, John Winthrop. It appears well organized. The docks are crowded. As many as a thousand people – men, women (several who are noticeably with child), and children of all ages – are making this journey to the New World. There are so many of us that the *Arabella* is only one of four ships in our little fleet. Excitement is in the air, as well as fear – trans-Atlantic crossings are long and dangerous. And, there is regret and nostalgia. We're leaving our homes, farms, businesses, friends, sisters and brothers, and everything that is familiar and dear. We love our home in England, but since King Charles I took the throne five years ago our lives have grown increasingly hard. Our future here looks bleak for us Puritans.

Since the death of Charles' father, James I, in 1625, it all seems a whirlwind. James ruled with a light hand – some would say hesitant and uneasy hand. We tolerated him and he us. We desire a true reform in the Church of England and a purer church, hence the name given us, Puritans. It's been almost a century since King Henry VIII broke from Rome, and according to our reading of the Holy Scriptures, there are far too many vestiges of Roman Catholicism lingering in the English church. We, along with our brethren Presbyterians in Scotland, believe that our souls are saved only by faith in the Lord Jesus Christ. Through faith in his resurrection, Christ, by His grace, forgives all of our sins. We have no need to confess our sins to a priest. We confess only to God and see ourselves as a "priesthood of all believers." We also believe that the Sovereign Lord God Almighty has elected or predestined some men and women for salvation. We don't know who these people are; only God knows them until their salvation is revealed. Therefore, we work for a just, merciful, and righteous society in strict accordance with the Bible's teachings so that as the Apostle Paul said to the Athenians on Mars Hill, everyone *would seek him and perhaps reach out for him and find him, though he is not far from any one of us.* (Acts 17:27) These beliefs puts us at odds with "high church" clergy in the Church of England and in opposition to Catholic doctrine.

While James was on the throne, we more or less got along. James commissioned the scholars at Westminster to translate the Bible that now bears his name as the King James Bible. But, this new king is not his father! Charles, less than a year into his reign, married a French princess, Henrietta Maria of the Royal House of Bourbon. They were married – he by proxy not even bothering to show up for his own wedding! – in front of the church doors at the Cathedral of Notre Dame in Paris. When we heard this news, our hearts sank. Would this new king and his Catholic queen drag us back under the dominion of the Roman pope? When we saw how heavy-handed Charles was with Parliament, shutting it down and ordering new taxes without Parliament's consent, we knew things would only get worse for us. John Winthrop, our leader, who was a king's commissioner of revenue in London lost his position. Why? Because he is a Puritan. After five years of this, the New World – New England to be specific – looks to be the Promised Land.

Plymouth Planation is now ten years old, and we will add to their numbers in order to build a godly society, where righteousness under the Lord God's law flourishes. That's why we're here on the docks boarding these ships. The captain has ordered everyone aboard and the sailors are preparing to hoist sails. As surely as God led the Children of Israel across the desert, God is leading us across the sea to America. But still our hearts are heavy. We know that we will never again see our beloved England, and only in the rare letter will we receive news from our families who remain here, but the time for lamenting these things is now passed. Behind us is England; in front of us is a new American horizon. All is in God's hands.

* * *

Around the time of the voyage, John Winthrop preached a sermon entitled "A Model of Christian Charity," which began with these words: "GOD ALMIGHTY in his most holy and wise providence, hath so disposed of the condition of mankind, as in all times some must be rich, some poor, some high and eminent in power and dignity; others mean and in submission."

The question that Winthrop raised is why? Why did God ordain such disparity among people's lives? It seems so unfair, capricious, and arbitrary. Winthrop gave three reasons why. First, it is the way that God ordered creation "for the preservation and good of the whole." In nature, the healthy forest has a variety of trees, and even within the same species of trees there is variety with some growing strong and tall and others languishing and small. The same is true of an ecosystem such as the ocean, and among land animals, herds such as bison and deer have individuals that are young and old, strong and weak, healthy and sick, aggressive and gentle.

Winthrop sees the same pattern in human society as well, believing it is the way God ordained all of nature. Is it fair or just? It is neither; it is simply the way things are. Second, when it comes to people, these differences are there to "manifest the work of his Spirit." God's Spirit is manifested when the poor are fed, law-breakers are justly punished, goodness prevails, and society is decent, moral, and orderly. These things and additional benevolences are the work of the Spirit in God's people, who show His love by building a more perfect and righteous society. The third and final reason that Winthrop gave for the disparity among people is the most profound. It is so "that every man might have need of others, and from hence they might be all knit more nearly together in the Bonds of brotherly affection." In our dependence upon one another we have the opportunity to live by Christ's command to *love one another*. (John 13:34) Winthrop saw that everyone needs to be loved and everyone needs to love.

Love one another even when some are mean and unlovable, and others good, gentle and easy to love. Love one another including the poor and weak, and not just the rich and powerful, who might advance you in some way. It is an impossibly high standard! To have any hope of achieving or even being near this standard, Winthrop believed that society must be both just and merciful. He said in his sermon that there must be a balance between justice and mercy. "There are two rules whereby we are to walk one towards another: Justice and Mercy." To treat one another justly and mercifully, God gave us "the law of nature and the law of grace, or the moral law or the law of the gospel," and the wisdom of Holy Scripture would be the Puritan's guide for just and merciful living.

To Winthrop justice and mercy were not lofty theological concepts that make for a high-sounding sermon. To him, justice and mercy were concrete, practical virtues that were to be demonstrated daily in how the Puritan's treated others in the community, and he knew that among neighbors giving, lending, and forgiving can be particularly hard. Therefore, he gave examples of justice and mercy during times of abundance and plenty, and in times of need. If a brother is in need, he said, "If thou lovest God thou must help him." Set within this context of giving and lending, Winthrop said that the first duty is to look after and provide for your own family, because it is within the family that dependency upon one another is first experienced and where children learn of love, duty, and personal responsibility to God and others. With their character so trained, then they will have the wisdom to know when and how to give and lend in order to best help someone. Regarding forgiveness, it should be readily offered, because Christ readily forgives us. Winthrop saw doing all these things as a "duty of mercy [being] exercised" and necessary for living into the requirements of the Golden Rule.

But, what about times of peril to the community as a whole? Should the Puritans live just and merciful lives when they are in mortal danger? Winthrop knew that danger and peril would surely come as they carved out farms and homes in the wilderness, and he also knew that disease and famine were likely, as everyone in England was familiar with the starving times in the Jamestown Colony, and the deadly attacks by Native Americans. Therefore, how were the Puritans to conduct themselves under such duress? Winthrop said, "The same as before, but with more enlargement towards others and less respect towards ourselves and own right." In other words, forget yourselves and what you consider are your rights and your privileges. For the good of the community, you are to be more loving, more just, and more merciful than before the hard times came. He said the Puritans in New England were to live as they did in the early church, and he cited the faith of saints throughout the ages. Continuing with the church as a model for their community, Winthrop said, "Ye are the body of Christ and members of the part. All the parts of this body being thus united... If one member suffers, all suffer with it. If one be in honor, all rejoice with it." And, knitting this body of Christ together is love. Winthrop said, "This love among Christians is a real thing, not imaginary. This love is a divine, spiritual, nature; free, active, strong, courageous, permanent, undervaluing all things beneath its proper object and of all the graces, this make us nearer to resemble the virtues of our Heavenly Father."

Winthrop concluded his lengthy sermon, urging them to live together in New England "in all meekness, gentleness, patience and liberality." If they did these things then, "The Lord will be our God, and delight to dwell among us, as in one people, and will command a blessing upon us in all our ways. So that we shall see much more of his wisdom, power, goodness and truth, than formerly we have been acquainted with. We shall find that the God of Israel is among us, when ten of us shall be able to resist a thousand of our enemies; when he shall make us a praise and glory that men shall say of succeeding plantations, 'the Lord make it like that of New England.' For we must consider that we shall be a city upon a hill."

It's uncertain if Winthrop preached "A Model of Christian Charity" sermon aboard the *Arabella* during the Atlantic crossing or the evening before the Puritans boarded the ship for New England. What is known is that they arrived in Boston Harbor in June 1630. Fearing if they settled in one main community that an attack by Native Americans might wipe-out the entire colony, they spread out and established smaller communities around the harbor and along the Charles River. These settlements would become Boston, Roxbury, Cambridge, Charlestown, Medford, and others. Approximately, two hundred of the roughly one thousand died that first year succumbing primarily to disease. John Winthrop served several terms as governor of the colony, and in the years between 1630 to 1640, thousands more Puritans would make the journey to New England.

Today, Americans are four centuries removed from Winthrop's "A Model of Christian Charity" sermon. What are we 21st Century Americans to make of Winthrop's words? The phrase "a city upon a hill" is well known and quoted in important speeches. Before departing Boston to take the Oath of Office as President of the United States, John F. Kennedy gave a speech to Massachusetts lawmakers in the State House on January 9, 1961. As president-elect, he, like John Winthrop four hundred years earlier, was on the threshold of governing. Winthrop in his sermon articulated the principles by which the Puritans should live and be governed. What of Kennedy? By what principles should 20th Century Americans live and be governed?

In his speech, the president-elect said, "Today the eyes of all people are truly upon us – and our governments, in every branch, at every level, national, state and local, must be as a city upon a hill – constructed and inhabited by men aware of their great trust and their great responsibilities." Then, like Winthrop, Kennedy quoted the Bible saying that "for those to whom much is given, much is required." (Luke 12:48) And, for those men, who are given much and govern, Kennedy asked by what criteria will history judge them, including himself? He answered saying, "Firstly, were we truly men of courage... Secondly, were we truly men of judgment... Thirdly, were we truly men of integrity... Finally, were we truly men of dedication... Courage – judgment – integrity – dedication... these are the qualities which, with God's help, this son of Massachusetts hopes will characterize our government's conduct in the four stormy years that lie ahead." The storm that lay, not just ahead, but was already upon America was the Cold War with the Soviet Union. In Kennedy's speech, we hear echoes of Puritan values. Almost thirty years later, on his way out of office, President Reagan harkened back to the Puritans and Winthrop's sermon. Reagan referred to America as a "shining city upon a hill." Soon, after he left office, the Cold War was finally over, and the 21st Century was only a decade away.

In both the Kennedy and Reagan speeches, we see that modern politicians like the lofty idea of America as "a city upon a hill," a model for all the world, which indeed America is or perhaps sadly was. But, "a city upon a hill" was only the punch line of Winthrop's sermon. In choosing this phrase from Jesus' Sermon on the Mount, Winthrop was encouraging the Puritans to strive for a godly, virtuous, moral, decent, just, and merciful society. To achieve this goal, he implored the Puritans, as they established their colony in New England, to lead humble and meek lives in obedience to God's laws. If they did, God would bless them and they would inherit the land. Yet, the words humility and meekness appear infrequently in the sermon. Instead, Winthrop preached on justice, mercy, love, and forgiveness, and in his speech, President Kennedy spoke of courage, judgment, integrity, and dedication. All these are virtues, and virtues are like robust and beautiful flowers, growing in rich and verdant garden soil. The soil – in fact the only soil – in which virtue blooms is humility. All virtues are rooted in humility.

The 19th Century theologian, writer, and pastor, Andrew Murray, wrote: "The life God bestows is imparted not once for all, but each moment continuously, by the unceasing operation of his mighty power. Humility, the place of entire dependence on God, is, from the very nature of things, the first duty and the highest virtue of the creature, and the root of every virtue. And so pride, or the loss of this humility, is the root of every sin and evil." ("Humility & Absolute Surrender," p. 6) Therefore, humility is indeed the spiritual soil, the *humus*, from which all virtue – faith, hope, love, justice, mercy, courage, perseverance, gratitude, and more – grows. Conversely, pride is the soul's spiritual substance from which all vice comes.

No farm crop – be it wheat or corn, soybean or cotton, lettuce or asparagus – grows in the soil unless it is the will of the farmer. So it is with either virtue or vice growing in our souls. Our will determines the crop that grows, and human will is determined by the simplest of decisions. Do we accept our dependency upon God or not? Both Winthrop in his 1630 sermon and Murray 300 years later in his book told us that dependency upon God is the starting point for humility and pride is rejection of that dependency. Inherent in Winthrop's understanding of creation is a dependency upon God that is incumbent upon every man and woman. Flowing from this dependency upon God is a dependency upon one another, which was of vital importance for establishing cities in a wilderness. Winthrop said it was necessary "that every man might have need of others." Andrew Murray also knew the truth about dependency upon God. In his quote above, he said, "Humility, the place of entire dependence on God, is... the first duty... of the creature." From dependency upon God comes humility from humility comes all the virtues from the virtues comes a society that is "a city upon a hill."

Certainly today America's cities are decaying, and slowly Americans are beginning to realize that the condition of our cities is a reflection of what is in our souls. Generation after generation of Americans have been taught to reject dependency upon God, and with God eliminated, only self remains. In our arrogance, Americans, like Adam and Eve, believe that we can be gods and gods don't need anyone or anything. In our prideful arrogance, we have rejected the very things that made the Puritans, and by extension Americans, so remarkably successful. We have rejected God, brotherly love, and the mutual dependency that binds a nation together. Pride, not humility, is in the American soul, and without humility, none of the other virtues grow.

Meanwhile, vice flourishes. Crime, drug addiction, violence –
sadly these vices and many others define America's largest cities.
For decades we have attempted to solve these problems with
government programs based on the latest results from university
studies. Yet, the problems not only persist, but increase. No new
government program or results from the latest university research
will solve any of America's urban problems. When new things
don't work, it's time to return to old things that did. It's time for
America to believe again Winthrop's vision for a new society
built on humility. When Americans believe that the meek are
blessed and *will inherit the earth,* then, once again America
"shall be a city upon a hill."

Chapter 3.
FAITH... awakened and mountains moved

Jesus along with Peter, James, and John approached a crowd arguing with the other nine disciples. When the crowd saw Jesus walking toward them, they ran to meet him, and Jesus asked, *"What are you arguing about?"* (Mark 9:16) A man in the crowd answered that he had brought his son to the disciples and asked them to heal him. The father said that his son had suffered seizures since childhood. When convulsed, the boy would fall to the ground and foam at the mouth. In the past, the child had fallen into fire and water and had to be rescued. The father said that the disciples tried to heal his son, but they couldn't. The father then said to Jesus:

"But if you can do anything, take pity on us and help us."

23 *"'If you can'?"* *said Jesus. "Everything is possible for one who believes."*

24 *Immediately the boy's father exclaimed, "I do believe; help me overcome my unbelief!"*

25 *When Jesus saw that a crowd was running to the scene, he rebuked the impure spirit. "You deaf and mute spirit," he said, "I command you, come out of him and never enter him again."*

26 *The spirit shrieked, convulsed him violently and came out. The boy looked so much like a corpse that many said, "He's dead." 27 But Jesus took him by the hand and lifted him to his feet, and he stood up.*

28 *After Jesus had gone indoors, his disciples asked him privately, "Why couldn't we drive it out?"*

29 *He replied, "This kind can come out only by prayer."* Mark 9:22-29)

Matthew's account of this event is the same except for Jesus' response to the disciples' question regarding their lack of success in healing the boy. Matthew records this exchange as follows: *19 Then the disciples came to Jesus in private and asked, "Why couldn't we drive it out?"*

20 He replied, "Because you have so little faith. Truly I tell you, if you have faith as small as a mustard seed, you can say to this mountain, 'Move from here to there,' and it will move. Nothing will be impossible for you." (Matthew 17:19-21)

The Greek word for "seizure" translates literally as "moonstruck." Considering the state of 1st Century medical science, describing the child's episodic *grand mal* seizures as being moonstruck or demonic is expected. However, the underlying medical diagnosis as to the cause of the boy's seizures is not the point the gospel writers were making when they memorialized this event in scripture. The failure of the nine disciples and Jesus having to heal the boy contrasts the weakness of disbelief with the power of faith. Jesus seemed irritated that the father said, *"If you can do anything..."* What more could Jesus do to demonstrate his authority and power? The blind could see, the deaf could hear, the lame could walk, and the dead had been restored to life. The father asked Jesus to help him overcome his unbelief, and Jesus healed the boy. But, our Lord's response to his disciples was more pointed. After all, they had witnessed Jesus' miracles firsthand, and he had invested in them the power and authority to heal. Mark tells us that he instructed them to pray; prayer strengthens faith. Matthew provides us with Jesus' teaching on the power of faith; even faith as small as a mustard seed can move a mountain.

We are two thousand years removed from Jesus' healing of this boy and his open disappointment with his disciples' lack of faith. In today's world, how are we to take Jesus' statement that *if you have faith as small as a mustard seed, you can say to this mountain, 'Move from here to there,' and it will move. Nothing will be impossible for you."* Really? Nothing will be impossible for a person of faith? Perhaps, Jesus meant this to be a proverbial statement, meaning that you'll be surprised at just how much you can accomplish. Or, maybe we should take Jesus at his word, and with just a small amount of faith we can move something as large as a mountain. Let's go now to 18th Century British colonial America to see if faith can really move a mountain. Our story begins in the winter of 1736 aboard a wooden sailing ship named the *Simmonds* that is bound for the new city of Savannah in the Georgia colony.

* * *

Somewhere in the Atlantic off the coast of the Colony of Georgia, January 1736

The *Simmonds* was a typical early 18th Century sailing ship that hauled cargo and ferried passengers between Britain and her growing and prosperous American colonies. In October 1735, the passengers boarded, the cargo was loaded, and the *Simmonds* set sail. Now, in late January after three months at sea, they still had not reached Savannah. Worse, the ship had the bad luck of sailing through several Atlantic winter storms. It wasn't certain – it never was in this era of sailing – that those aboard the *Simmonds* would ever see land again.

Among the passengers was a group of Moravian Brethren from Herrnhut in the Saxony region of Germany. The Brethren trace their origins back to 1415, and the early and important church reformer, John Hus (1369-1415). A Czech, Hus a was professor of philosophy at the University of Prague. A century before Martin Luther, Professor Hus was questioning Roman Catholic Church doctrine. Inspired by the writings of John Wycliffe, Hus developed an interest in scripture, and began pointing out where the church diverged from scripture. His work contributed to Luther's writing of the 95 theses, and it also got him burned at the stake as a heretic. After his death, the Brethren formed and endured, but early in the 18th Century, a persecution arose against them in their Czech homeland. Seeing their plight, the leaders of Saxony (in today's Germany) gave them refuge and they settled in an area they called Herrnhut which in the Czech language means "the Lord protects."

This group of Brethren aboard the *Simmonds* were missionaries on their way to the Georgia colony. They were attracted by the work of James Oglethorpe (1696-1785), an English soldier and Member of Parliament, who was granted a charter to create a colony that would give prisoners, the poor, and outcast a new start. As a Member of Parliament, Oglethorpe served on a "Gaol Committee" that investigated conditions in England's debtor prisons. What Oglethorpe found appalled him, and he set himself to the task of giving the poor a fresh start in the New World. In February 1733, he dropped anchor in the Savannah River, and with convicts from debtors' prisons, he began to build a beautiful city named after the river. Now, just three years later, Moravian Brethren were sending missionaries to work and help in this bold endeavor of Christian mercy and charity. Also, among the passengers was a 33 year-old Oxford educated Anglican clergyman, who was going to the Georgia colony for the same reason – to serve the poor, minister to the English settlers, and share the gospel message – the Good News – of Jesus Christ with the Native Americans.

The Anglican minister, who was a slightly built man, was in awe of the Moravian Brethren. During a particularly bad nighttime storm, he had been terrified that at any moment, as the ship creaked and groaned, pitched and rolled in heavy seas, he would meet a watery death. Yet, the Moravian missionaries, who were traveling as family groups with women and children, appeared calm and serene. At the roughest and most gut-wrenching parts of the storm, they even sang hymns. Did they not care that their children could easily drown at sea?

The *Simmonds* survived the storm, but it had been powerful enough to snap the main mast, which, the next morning, the crew was busily repairing. On deck, the fearful clergyman spotted a Brethren. Unable to contain his curiosity any longer, he asked the Brethren if he had been at all frightened during the storm. He responded with a simple, "No."

The clergyman appeared puzzled, and asked. "Weren't your women and children afraid?"

"No," the man responded, "our women and children are not afraid to die."

The Anglican minister was John Wesley (1703-1791), and the Moravian Brethren's faith in God and the peace that ensued from it contrasted sharply with his lack of faith and resulting fear. This moment made a life-changing impression on Wesley, and he wrote in his journal, "This is the most glorious day I have ever seen." Church historian, Bruce Shelley, observed that Wesley at this time, "had a form of godliness, but he had yet to find its power." (Shelley, "Church History in Plain Language," p. 346) It would be another two years before Wesley would experience the New Testament's power of the Holy Spirit.

A line from the popular Thanksgiving hymn "We Gather Together" says, "He [the Lord] chastens and hastens his will to make to known." Wesley was chastened. He had witnessed aboard the *Simmonds* a remarkable testament of faith, but he was like the father of the boy, who suffered seizures. He still had reservations about the power of faith, and God's will for his life was unknown. What transpired in Georgia was a period of more chastening and hastening. Wesley fell in love with Sophy Hopkey, who was the 18 year-old daughter of Savannah's chief magistrate. She eventually married another man, and Wesley, the spurned suitor, reacted by banning the newlyweds from receiving communion, which created turmoil in the church and community. Further complicating the young minister's life was that his work among the Native Americans was not progressing as he envisioned. After two years, emotionally drained and spiritually uncertain, Wesley returned to England in February 1738. On the voyage home, he wrote, "I went to America to convert the Indians, but, oh, who shall convert me?" Ashamed of his behavior and uncertain of what he believed, he pondered what to do next.

What a sad state of affairs! Wesley was the son of an Anglican minster. His mother had a strong influence on his moral upbringing and had instilled in him the discipline of living a perfect Christian life. At Oxford University, he had been elected a fellow in Lincoln College, and had joined a pious group of students who gathered for Bible study and prayer. His younger brother, Charles, had organized this group, who called themselves by various names including "The Holy Club," and "The Methodists." Now this! Wesley was back in England and where was this perfect Christian life he was supposed to live? Georgia had been a disaster, but there was one point of light in that experience: the faith of the Moravian Brethren. What did they have or know that he didn't? In London, he found Peter Bohler, a Moravian pastor.

Although he had spent hours in prayer, had dedicated himself to Bible study, had the zeal to be a missionary, and had rarely missed Holy Communion, Wesley was religious and godly yet lacking and wanting. He could teach an Englishman how to be a good Anglican, but he had no power to save a Native American's soul. Where was the faith that moved mountains? Bohler counseled Wesley that he needed to be reborn. He told him that justification by faith was not merely a doctrine of the church, but that it was knowledge that Christ had forgiven him, John Wesley, personally for his sins. Wesley soon experienced this forgiveness. On May 24, 1738, he wrote in his journal: "I felt that I did trust in Christ. Christ alone, for salvation; and an assurance was given me that he had taken away *my* sins, even *mine*, and saved me from the law of sin and death." Wesley was reborn and soon America and Europe would similarly be reborn. The Great Awakening was underway. Faith was moving a mountain!

While traveling from London to Oxford, Wesley read of Jonathan Edwards and the miraculous revival taking place in New England. The movement of the Holy Spirit in New England had a great influence on Wesley. Soon, he met with George Whitefield, who also had been a missionary to Georgia. Whitefield now back in England was preaching to thousands of coalminers and their families in Bristol, but not in churches. Whitefield preached in open fields. And, just like Edwards' experience in New England, the Holy Spirit was moving in Bristol through the clear and strong voice of George Whitefield, who urged Wesley to join him. But, Wesley, the Oxford scholar and gentleman, and only recently a born again Christian, was reluctant to give up what he found comfortable. He wrote, "Having been all my life so tenacious of every point relating to decency and order, I should have thought the saving of souls almost a sin if it had not been done in a church." But, Wesley did join Whitefield and he too was given the power to speak to thousands in fields and pastures and hundreds in churches. Souls were saved, because the fire of the Holy Spirit was lit within him. Faith was moving a mountain of humanity!

In 1739, George Whitefield returned to the American colonies and preached from Georgia to Massachusetts. The response to his preaching in the colonies was the same as in England; thousands were saved. The Wesley brothers, John and Charles, who remained in England were experiencing the same result. On both sides of the Atlantic, the Great Awakening was reaching full bloom. It began in the 1730s and lasted well into the

1740s. Wesley, Edwards, and Whitefield were leading evangelists in the Awakening, but it was a much longer list of individuals, churches, and denominations that participated in this quickening of the soul by the Holy Spirit and the effect was profound.

In fields and pastures, barns and factories, individuals heard the gospel message and experienced the salvation of Jesus Christ. Certainly, churches were involved and denominations too, but this wasn't the top down salvation that John Wesley had known in the Church of England. No, this was grassroots; a bottom up salvation of individuals who then shaped churches, society, and government. In England at the time of his death in 1791, it was estimated that Wesley had preached 40,000 sermons, and approximately 79,000 followed his approach to worship and Christian living that was (and still is) called Methodism. In America during the 1790s, there were around 40,000 Methodists. Other denominations and churches were experiencing similar growth. This was the Great Awakening, a new birth in the Spirit of God, and this new found faith in Christ had ripple effects throughout society particularly in America.

In Europe, vestiges of Christendom remained. Christendom was a centuries-long period of time where the one church, the Roman Catholic Church, influenced and guided every aspect of life from the monarchy, i.e., the government, to society, and to the family. Taxes and the monarchy supported the Church, and the Church in turn participated in secular affairs. The Reformation, however, and the ensuing conflicts, shattered Christendom, but the practice of state supported churches did not end. England had the Church of England which was Anglican, and Scotland had the Church of Scotland that was Presbyterian. Among the Germanic states, depending in part upon the region, you were either Lutheran or Catholic, and France until the French Revolution retained the Roman Catholic Church as the state church. In America, as the colonies grew and attracted various Christian faiths, a single state supported church simply would never work. Plus, the Great Awakening was a revival movement that transcended churches and denominations.

Men and women understood themselves to be individuals, who are directly accountable to God; not the state church. Christ died for their individual sins. It was by their faith in Christ that their sins were forgiven. America was a new experience of the individual and faith in God without the encumbrance of a state church that was favored by the king and supported by taxes. This separation of church and state required a new way of governing, and this new way included an understanding that salvation is not granted by the church, but by faith in Christ, and rights are granted not by a king, but by God and these rights included freedom of religion, freedom of speech, freedom of assembly, and all the rights that are hallmarks of America. These ideas and this new way of thinking flowed directly into the preamble of the Declaration of Independence. Such radical ideas regarding individual rights and freedoms were not directly part of the Great Awakening. The movement, however, fostered the understanding of the individual as responsible to God, and from there it's a short step that rights and freedom are granted by God, not the government.

In July 1776, after the Declaration of Independence was signed, Thomas Jefferson, John Adams, and Benjamin Franklin were assigned the task of designing what would become the Seal of the United States of America. Their early designs involved biblical imagery. Franklin wanted to feature Moses looking on as Pharaoh's chariots became trapped in a watery grave. Jefferson wanted the Seal to show the Children of Israel crossing the desert. This identification of the new American experience with the Exodus story is because the Founders saw parallels in the stories. In the Exodus, God prepared the hearts of people by sending

Moses and then teaching them who he [God] is. While God was preparing hearts, he was also crushing Pharaoh, the mightiest king in the world. In America, God sent the Great Awakening to prepare hearts and teach who Christ is. The expectation was that God working, through the American Revolution would crush King George III, the mightiest ruler in the world. Further, just as the Children of Israel crossed the desert to live in a new nation under God, Christians had crossed the Atlantic. This is what Jefferson and Franklin were seeking to capture in the Seal.

In the end, the biblical imagery did not win out, but the Latin inscription on the Seal does point to God's hand in the founding. The full inscription reads:

E PLURIBUS UNUM – ANNUIT COEPTIS – MDCCLXXVI –
NOVUS ORDO SECLORUM

Shelley, the church historian, translates the Latin as follows: "One out of many – (God) has smiled on our undertakings – 1776 – a new order of (or for) the ages." In the decades leading up to the revolution, Americans from diverse backgrounds (the many) converged to a consensus (the one), and the consensus was that they will stand as individuals before God to be judged. However, through faith, Jesus Christ will grant pardon for sins, and because Christ was resurrected from death so shall be the individual. This consensus mindset was a direct result of the Great Awakening, and it spilled over into thinking about governance. If you're an individual judged by God, and loved by Christ, then government's claim on you as an individual is secondary – almost trivial! This thinking is expressed in the Declaration of Independence and Bill of Rights regarding rights granted by God, and government's role is to secure and protect those rights. Such thinking was – and is still today – breathtakingly revolutionary. It is for the ages, and this is what America's Founders sought to convey in the nation's Seal.

Can faith as small as a mustard seed move a mountain? One of the hardest things to move is the human heart yet tens of thousands of hearts were moved and turned toward Christ in the Great Awakening, and from that awakening, truly a mountain was moved. That mountain was the way nations are governed and the concept of natural rights, i.e., rights given to all people by God. From this movement in thinking, the United States was born and the world was changed! Indeed, faith can move a mountain!

Today, America, both in time and spirit, is far removed from the Great Awakening. Christians and churches are like the father of the boy, who suffered seizures. He doubted Jesus saying, "*[I]f you can do anything...*" And, Americans are like John Wesley, who on the *Simmonds*, was astounded by the faith of the Moravian Brethren. Wesley was highly educated and self-assured about what he believed, but he did not have faith in God. Yet, when he found it, the power of the Spirit of Christ, working through him changed the world and that same power, working in the father, healed the boy with seizures. When the virtue of faith is awakened, mountains are moved!

Jesus said, "*[I]f you have faith as small as a mustard seed, you can say to this mountain, 'Move from here to there,' and it will move. Nothing will be impossible for you.*"

Source: Bruce L. Shelley, Church History in Plain Language, 4th Ed., Published by Thomas Nelson, 2008, p. 346-356.

Chapter 4.
HOPE... revived in a wilderness

⁵ Then the family heads of Judah and Benjamin, and the priests and Levites—everyone whose heart God had moved— prepared to go up and build the house of the Lord in Jerusalem. (Ezra 1:5)

Wilderness comes in many forms. There are geographical wildernesses. A desert, a rugged mountaintop, an uninhabited topical island, and a heavily forested river valley of virgin timber are some examples of wilderness landscapes. Living in any one of these environments presents physical and even life threatening challenges. There are also societal wildernesses, where things of merit, goodness, charity, compassion, mercy, delight, light-heartedness, and laughter scarcely exist and daily living is a grind that wears on the soul much as the geographical wilderness wears on the body. Blighted, economically poor urban areas can be societal wildernesses, but this type of wilderness knows no limits. Social groups as small as families can be societal wildernesses, where appropriate and healthy interactions, entertainment, hobbies, and endeavors are entirely absent and individuals are as trapped as they would be on a deserted island. Then, there are personal wildernesses of the heart, mind, and soul. Personal wildernesses, like the geographical and societal, comes in many fashions yet they share a commonality. Personal wildernesses are barren spiritual landscapes, where our thirsty hearts and restless minds find no rest or comfort. Spiritual landscapes can be more frightening, and uniquely challenging as any geographical wilderness. Each of these wildernesses, whether geographical, societal, or personal, share a common element; deep loneliness. The geographical physically separates, the societal emotionally separates, and the personal spiritually separates our being from

God, others, and our surroundings. When trapped in a wilderness of any kind, where does one find hope?

In the verse above, *the family heads of Judah and Benjamin, and the priests and Levites* were certainly not in a geographical wildness. In fact, they were living in ancient Babylon, home of the famed Hanging Gardens that sat adjacent to King Nebuchadnezzar's palace that was described as "The Marvel of Mankind." Yet in the midst of this splendor, they were trapped in societal and personal wildernesses. The year was 538 B.C., and for nearly a half-century, the Jews had been held captive in Babylon.

In 586 B.C., the Babylonians under King Nebuchadnezzar looted the Temple in Jerusalem of all its treasures and then destroyed the magnificent building that Solomon had built 300 years earlier. The Temple was God's House. The Presence of the Lord God resided above the Ark of the Covenant inside the Holy of Holies. Every Jew, no matter how unfaithful or flagrantly uncaring they were about their faith, knew the significance of the Temple; their entire society was organized around worship in the Temple. Now, it was gone and so were they. They now lived as captives in a distant land, whose culture and gods were alien to them. Surely, the Jewish heart, mind, and soul existed in a depressing personal wilderness. God had abandoned them – His people – to the Babylonians. Who were they now? Where was God? They were lonely creatures separated from their Creator. Then amazingly, hope came into their wildernesses.

It came unexpectedly, like flowering crocuses pushing through the late winter snow. The verse above says, *everyone whose heart God had moved.* When it seems winter will never end, God brings forth a palette of spring colors, and so it was with the hearts of captive Israel. God moved hearts and suddenly hope blossomed in their wildernesses. The Children of Israel would return to the Promised Land. The Temple would be rebuilt. God would make it so. He had not abandoned his people forever. In their wildernesses, he revived hope.

What about today? None of the wildernesses have gone away. In fact, societal and personal wildernesses in America today are as dark and forbidding as ever. Where is hope? Where is God? Do either still exist for Americans today? To answer these questions, we are going to Kentucky. Our first stop will be in 1801, when the Kentucky Territory was a geographical wilderness, as well as societal and personal wildernesses. Yet in this challenging trifecta of wildernesses, God moved hearts and gave hope to Kentuckians. Our second and final stop will also be in Kentucky in the year 2020, and once there, we will hear stories of God moving hearts. Let's go now to the land of Daniel Boone.

* * *

Cane Ridge, Kentucky Territory, August 1801.

The first wagons began arriving early morning on Thursday, August 6. It was so early in fact that the summer sun was still hidden behind Cane Ridge so named by Daniel Boone, because a cane plant similar to bamboo covered the ridge. By midmorning the pasture was filling with wagons and people setting up camp yet the event didn't officially start until tomorrow, Friday, the 7th. The people were frontiersmen, and whether farmers, hunters, trappers or a bit of all three, they shared a common characteristic. Men, women, children, and even babies, who were loosely and carelessly slung on the hips of older siblings, all had this trait. They were as roughhewn as the log cabins in which they lived. They knew how to survive in the Kentucky wilderness, and they had no time for nonsense, fakery, or fraud. Cheat at a card game and the tip of a Bowie knife would quickly be pressed on your Adam's apple, and it wouldn't be withdrawn until all ill-gotten gains were forfeited. Yet here they were on this warm summer morning in Cane Ridge, while back home, which included every corner of the Kentucky Territory, summer crops were left untended, and livestock were fed and watered, milked and pastured by a disappointed few, who had no choice but to remain behind – farms don't run themselves. Still they kept arriving! When the event was over, an estimated 20,000 had participated, which was about ten percent of the territory's population. Why? What could possibly possess a hard-scrabble people to leave busy farms, come to Cane Ridge, and camp in a pasture for almost a week? It was nothing less than the Spirit of God.

The Apostle John in his gospel reports a nighttime conversation between Jesus and a Pharisee named Nicodemus. Jesus told this highly educated teacher of the law that in order to see the kingdom of God a person must be born again. (John 3) Nicodemus took Jesus literally and had no idea how a grown man could reenter the womb, and Jesus answered him saying, *Flesh gives birth to flesh, but the Spirit gives birth to spirit. [7] You should not be surprised at my saying, 'You must be born again.' [8] The wind blows wherever it pleases. You hear its sound, but you cannot tell where it comes from or where it is going. So it is with everyone born of the Spirit."* (John 3:6-8) So it was with Kentucky at the dawn of the 19th Century. Like a gentle breeze that moves the most massive of ships, the Spirit of God was moving the stony hearts of frontier people and this heavenly wind was propelling them to Cane Ridge to be born again. It had happened before. Just last year in Logan County, Kentucky near the Tennessee border, the fresh and cleansing breeze of the Holy Spirit blew.

In 1797 James McGready, a Presbyterian minister, arrived in Logan County. He had led congregations in North Carolina, and when Daniel Boone blazed a trail west through the Cumberland Gap into to Kentucky, McGready followed. By 1800, he was well established in the rapidly growing wilderness settlements. Other churches were being added as the population grew, and the pastors of these churches met to discuss ministering to the needs of these hardened settlers.

We think of the Wild West as being west of the Mississippi – Texas, Oklahoma, Colorado, and Arizona come to mind – but at the dawn of the 19th Century, Kentucky was the wild west. In 1790, the population was about 73,000. The 1800 census showed that the population had tripled in ten years to over 220,000. The hardship of the wilderness, the lust for opportunity, the constant influx of newly arrived rootless settlers, little to no law enforcement, an abundance of moonshine, and the attraction of gambling fueled societal and personal wildernesses in the midst of a geographical wilderness. This was the Kentucky trifecta, and in its wake were abandoned families, alcoholism, domestic abuse, bankruptcy, and violence. The pastors prayed for ways out of these wildernesses and for hope. And, God answered with the wind of His Spirit. As Jesus said to Nicodemus, *The wind blows wherever it pleases. You hear its sound, but you cannot tell where it comes from or where it is going. So it is with everyone born of the Spirit."* Where the Spirit is going is known only to God, but where the Spirit has been cannot be hidden. The Spirit of God came to Logan County in June 1800.

Since arriving in Logan County, Reverend McGready had observed the Scottish sacrament, whose roots date back to the 16th Century and the Scottish Reformation. The sacrament, whose focus is the Lord's Supper, was a multiple day event that was held outside during the summer months. How the Scottish sacrament was practiced varied, but it typically lasted from a Friday to a Monday, and some instances even days longer. On Friday, participants fasted until the afternoon and then only a light meal was taken. The emphasis in sermons, hymns, and prayers was on soul-searching, and knowing true humility before God. Saturday was a day of preparation for receiving communion on Sunday. Sermons, hymns, and prayers on this day included the attributes of a Christian life, God's righteous wrath and judgment of sinners, and the abundant saving grace of Jesus Christ. This day of preparation emphasized the solemnity and significance of partaking in the Lord's Supper. In fact, in order to receive communion, participants needed a communion token that was the size of a coin and usually made of lead.

Tokens were often stamped with scripture or "Do This In Remembrance of Me." Elders were responsible for dispensing them. If the person requesting a communion token was known to have been baptized and was demonstrably living a Christian life, the token was readily given. If the person was unknown and/or this was their first communion, then the elders would examine the applicant to ensure that they understood the meaning of the Lord's Supper, that they had repented, and desired to be born again. If unbaptized, they could be baptized that day and receive communion on Sunday. If, however, the elders were not convinced, the token was denied and the person urged to further examine themselves. It was not unusual for a person to be denied communion, and to prevent a token-less person from receiving the sacrament, a fence was placed around the communion table and the token was required for admittance. Sunday, of course, was the day of worship and communion, and on Monday a grand celebratory feast was held.

McGready along with other Presbyterian and Methodist pastors in the area decided to observe a Scottish sacrament in June 1800 on the grounds of the Red River Meeting House, which was a large log cabin used by the Presbyterians for worship. The observance proceeded as expected until Monday, the feast day. It was then that the Holy Spirit came. During the final worship service in the meeting house, a woman stood, shouted, and then sat down. All was silent for a moment, then one of the pastors felt a power come over him and sat down on the floor in front of the pulpit. The woman shouted again. Others began to shout, weep, and tremble. Incredible energy gripped the congregation with some shaking, having "the jerks" and others falling down. Someone shouted for them to stop that Presbyterians were orderly and did not abide this type of behavior, but they couldn't stop. The power of the Spirit of God was upon them, and they did not want to leave the meeting house. They were reborn! Alive, hopeful, energetic, and full of the Holy Spirit, they eventually went back to their homes reborn into a godly, moral life that was soon observed by their neighbors, and word of the events at the Red River Meeting House spread throughout the wilderness.

Just one month later in July, a second Scottish sacrament was held, and hundreds of people traveled long distances to attend. They came in wagons and camped on the church grounds, and here after the Scottish sacrament was called camp meetings. Camp meetings were held throughout the summer of 1800 with hundreds to thousands participating, and each was characterized by the presence of the Holy Spirit that was manifested by "the jerks," falling down, shouts, and glossolalia (speaking in tongues) brought about by an amazing energy that flowed in the congregation.

During the winter months, Reverend Barton Stone at Cane Ridge heard about the coming of the Holy Spirit to the Red River Meeting House. He described the events to his congregation, and to his astonishment, the mere description caused a surge of energy. They too began to shout, speak in tongues, and manifest signs of the Spirit. Afterwards, they were convinced that Cane Ridge should hold a camp meeting, and they began planning for the August 1801 meeting. In the movie "The Field of Dreams," the character played by James Earl Jones delivered a moving soliloquy that says in part, "... people will come... They'll come for reasons they can't even fathom." And so it was at Cane Ridge that August. People came, as did the Holy Spirit. All toll, it was estimated that around 20,000 participated in one or more days of the camp meeting. Historians identify the Cane River camp meeting and the numerous camp meetings leading up to it as the beginning of America's Second Great Awakening. It's estimated that around 100,000 Kentuckians, which was roughly half the population, participated in one or more camp meetings. Hope was revived in the wilderness. Kentucky and America were changed; reborn by the Spirit of God.

Today, the Cane Ridge camp meeting is more than 200 years old. What are we to make of it? Was it mere emotionalism, a form of group hysteria that even the no nonsense, down to earth farmers could not resist? Or was it real – a real coming of the Spirit of God that moved the hearts of a people, giving them hope and pushing back the wildernesses of their lives? Even in the 1800's this form of revival was not without critics. When the Holy Spirit was first manifested in the Red River Meeting House, there were shouts to stop – Presbyterians like order! But, history proves those critics were wrong, because from the seeming disorder of the camp meeting came a revival of hope that pushed back the wildernesses. Goodness, peace, and brotherly love pushed out the loneliness, division, and strife in families and communities. This change wasn't fleeting. It lasted. Yet still this was 200 years ago, and to better understand how the Holy Spirit speaks to and changes hearts, we need a more recent example of the coming of the Holy Spirit along with documentation of what happened in the revival and firsthand evidence of a sustained change in people's lives. Fortunately, we have such an example, and it is as recent as 2020. Let's go now to Wilmore, Kentucky.

* * *

Asbury University, Wilmore, Kentucky February 2020

In February 2020, we would all learn new words. They were coronavirus and COVID, and as these words were repeated over and over, the world became a dark wilderness of fear. It was a time of hopelessness, despair, and loneliness – the things found in all wildernesses. Yet, just as John's gospel says that a light shines in the darkness and the light cannot be overcome (John 1:5), so a light shone in this darkness. It was a light that was lit fifty years earlier in a small Methodist college in Wilmore, Kentucky, and a half-century later, no darkness has extinguished it.

In February 1970, the Holy Spirit came to Asbury College and remained there – never leaving, not for a second – for eight consecutive days. Fifty years later, Asbury University, as it is known today, commissioned a documentary video to tell the story of the revival, and interview participants to determine the lasting effects, if any, of their experience. (The video is readily available on YouTube.)

Days after the 1970 revival, as shown in the video, the president of Asbury College, Dr. Dennis F. Kinlow, held a press conference. With the events still quite fresh, he told the media, "You know as well as I that when it began there were a good many critics. There are many of us who, if we had been told this is the way God would come, we would say, 'No, that's not the way we want we him to come.' But, when he came something deep within the marrow of our bones spiritually responded that said, 'That's right.'" So, what did happen?

On Tuesday, February 3, 1970, Dr. Custer B. Reynolds, the Academic Dean, was scheduled to lead the regular weekly chapel service. Before the service, he said he felt that God was directing him not to speak. Instead, he was to invite anyone who desired to speak to come forward to the front of chapel and address the assembly. Later as he stood in the pulpit, Reynolds issued the invitation and a young man, who was in the senior class, slowly made his way to the front. He then described how he had wasted his four years at Asbury. His life had been a wilderness of sorts, filled with too many parties and too much of the trivial pursuits typical of college life. Now God was speaking to him, telling him to come home. His days in the spiritual wilderness were over. At that moment, the power of the Holy Spirit swept over the chapel. Dozens of students came forward, quickly filling the area in front of the pulpit. Some kneeled to pray, others gave their testimony, and still others confessed their sins and asked for forgiveness. And, no one – from those kneeling in the front to those sitting in the back pews – wanted to leave the chapel. Classes were cancelled, and when it was necessary to leave in order to eat or shower, they returned as quickly as possible.

For 8 days 24/7 this continued. Local Lexington news reported the events, and national TV networks and newspapers picked up the story. People from all over Kentucky, as well as Ohio, Indiana, and Michigan came to see and participate in this revival. Upon entering the chapel, people said they sensed the Presence of God that produced a range of emotions from fear to reverence to love to peace. The fear was not the adrenaline churning kind or the dreadful feeling of doom kind. Rather, it was the sense of being very near incredible power. This power engendered reverence, but the most important and distinct feeling was love – an overwhelming love that gave a deep sense of peace.

The Bible tell us that if we draw near to God, he will draw near to us. (James 4:8) In the Old Testament, God told the Jews, who were captive in Babylon, that if they would return to him, he would return to them. (Zechariah 1:3) They did, and God returned, moving hearts, and releasing them from their wilderness in Babylon to return to Jerusalem. Now, thousands of years later, the same thing was happening. Asbury students had been praying and seeking God. They returned to him, and he returned to them. For eight consecutive days in Asbury College chapel, the Spirit of God was there. When it was over, churches and colleges from around the nation requested that Asbury students come and tell about their experience. They did and in the summer of 1970, the revival spread, and its effects have lasted a half-century.

Asbury University's documentary video, entitled, "Deeper Still: Memories of God's Power and Love in the 1970 Asbury College Revival," interviewed numerous participants, and one was Sharon, who was a junior at the time of the revival. She recalled that the 1960's and '70's were a time of turmoil and despair. Young men, who were her age, were dying daily in the Vietnam War. The cultural revolution that was driven by drugs, sex, and rebellion against institutions, social conventions, and traditions was gaining momentum. Following the assassination of Dr. Martin Luther King in 1968, riots rocked cities and shook the nation. With these memories in mind, Sharon in 2020 said, "Everybody had a cause. A lot of anger and bitterness, and hatred [existed] in the culture overall. So, I think the revival was a piece of that [time period and it happened] to give us hope [and] to remind us that God is in control." Another woman, who was a student, remembered, "During the revival, the presence of the Holy Spirit was [so] real that I began to know that God loved me. If I never played another note on the piano or made another good grade that I didn't have to be anybody [other] than who I am. He loved me because He made me."

What is revival? Love. Love that changes lives. Love that says, "I know you. I made you. I will never abandon you. Return to me." Love that comes into all your wildernesses, revives hope, and brings a peace beyond understanding. These are the effects of the Spirit of God, and they are lasting. The things of this world bring trouble, turmoil, despair, and hopelessness. It is the way the world is and always has been. Yet, hope, love, beauty, and peace are but a breath away in a prayer. God will come. He may come powerfully in a large revival, or he may come quietly at your bedside, but he will definitely come, if only you have faith the size of a mustard seed, and where God is, there is hope – hope in this world, and hope for eternal life with God in the next.

In unexpected ways, the Spirit of God steps into our wildernesses, and where God is, there is love, hope, joy, and peace. God moved in the hearts of Jews living in the midst of the splendor and decadence ancient Babylon. That city in biblical times – and even to today – is symbolic of pride, greed, idolatry, and cruelty, and yet into this wilderness, the Spirit came. Hearts and minds were awakened, hope was revived, and the Jews returned to Jerusalem and rebuilt the Temple. God does not change, and what happened in ancient Babylon thousands of years ago, happened in Kentucky in the 1800s and again in 1970, and more recently in 2023 – again at Asbury University. Therefore, we should not be surprised by the coming of the Spirit, but we should expect the Spirit's coming for that is the virtue of hope!

Source: "Deeper Still: Memories of God's Power and Love in the 1970 Asbury College Revival," a production of The Epworth League @ 2019 The Epworth League.

Chapter 5.
LOVE... of God establishing a nation

The Apostle Paul wrote two letters to the church at Corinth. In the thirteenth chapter of the first letter, he penned a beautiful description of love.

⁴ Love is patient, love is kind. It does not envy, it does not boast, it is not proud. ⁵ It does not dishonor others, it is not self-seeking, it is not easily angered, it keeps no record of wrongs. ⁶ Love does not delight in evil but rejoices with the truth. ⁷ It always protects, always trusts, always hopes, always perseveres. Love never fails. (1st Corinthians 13:4-8)

Where do you find such an unselfish perfect love? We know from experience that we often are impatient, self-seeking, and keep score of wrongs. We harbor hurt feelings, dwell on slights, and then turn these wrong-headed things on the people that we profess to love. Where then is this perfect love that Paul is describing? It must be a love superior to the love experienced between say a husband and wife, a parent and child, or the closest of siblings and friends. The unfailing love that Paul had in mind is the love of the Lord God for his creatures, and this perfect love is found in Jesus Christ. Just a few verses later, the apostle refers to the perfect love of Christ by stating that *when perfection comes, the imperfect disappears.* (1st Corinthians 13:10) The imperfect love of this world disappears when Christ returns or when we enter the perfect love of heaven. But, we don't have to wait until the Second Coming or until we enter the heavenly realm to get glimpses of perfect love. To illustrate how we get images of perfect love in this life, Paul uses a mirror as a metaphor. He wrote:

[12] For now we see only a reflection as in a mirror; then we shall see face to face. Now I know in part; then I shall know fully, even as I am fully known. (1st Corinthians 13:12)

In the 1st Century, when Paul's letters to the Corinthians were written, the most expensive of mirrors could offer only flawed images. The highly polished bronze mirrors typical of that era were incapable of providing a true and detailed likeness. Throw in the fact that candles or oil lamps were the source of interior lighting, and the difficulty of clearly seeing reflected images becomes apparent. However, when standing face to face in bright sunlight, we can see all facial details, and Paul says the same will happen with perfect love. *We shall see face to face.* At that moment the love we now know in part, we shall know fully. One day, we will know Christ fully, and be known to Him fully, and that day will be when Christ returns or when we meet Him in heaven.

But, what of the here and now? Must we be reconciled to love that is inferior and imperfect? Sadly, our love for others and even for God is imperfect, and the love of others for us is imperfect as well. However, it is possible to love better, and Paul tells us how. He told the Corinthians to look in the mirror that reflects Christ's image. The Bible tells us who Christ is and the Holy Spirit confirms the truth of Christ. Therefore, we do have an image of Christ that we can hold up like a mirror. We won't get every detail right just as reflections in 1st Century bronze mirrors were blurry. Yet through our sinful eyes we have a clear enough picture of perfect love that we can do a much, much better job of loving perfectly right here and right now. We can love God more perfectly and then show that love to others more perfectly. It all depends upon us wanting to see Christ's love, and holding up the mirror so we can conform our lives to the image of his love.

So, how are we doing? Are we looking in that mirror and trying to love as Paul described? How's America doing? Are

Americans even looking in the mirror that reflects Christ's love, or are we looking in a different mirror that presents an image of love that bears no resemblance to Christ's love? Is what we call love today even love at all? To answer these questions, we're going back in time to the year 1787, and on this journey, we're going to identify the mirror that 18th Century Americans held up and how they patterned themselves according to the image of love that they saw. Then, we will compare the love of 18th Century Americans to what Americans call love today. Let's go now to Orange County, Virginia and begin our quest to understand the character of love American style.

* * *

Orange County, Virginia, Spring 1787

We're standing on the front portico of Montpelier, the home of the 4th U.S. president, James Madison. But, we're getting ahead of ourselves. It's 1787, no one has been president yet, because there is no Constitution. The governing document of the thirteen states is the Articles of Confederation, and it isn't working. The Articles, that were ratified in 1781 by the Continental Congress, were designed to ensure the independence and sovereignty of the states. To achieve this goal, the central government is very weak, and as a result, it is unable to effectively regulate commerce, conduct foreign affairs, tax, or impose tariffs. The rapidly growing, newly independent states need a workable central government, and for the past few years, Madison, Alexander Hamilton, and others have been lobbying to reform the Articles. A convention to discuss the matter has been called. It will take place a few weeks from now on May 25th in Philadelphia.

For months, Mr. Madison, who is 36 years old, has been holed up inside his stately 22 room brick plantation home. Montpelier is truly lovely especially in the spring, but Mr.

Madison and even his wife, Dolly, have scarcely been outside, because he has been hard at work in the library researching various forms of government. Reforming the Articles is not on his mind. He is drafting a framework for a new form of government that has come to be called the Virginia Plan. Only a close circle of friends that includes Thomas Jefferson and George Mason know what he's been working on. Most of the men, who have been elected by their states to serve as delegates to the Philadelphia convention, think the purpose is to amend the Articles of Confederation. When they arrive in Philadelphia, they will be surprised – even alarmed – to learn what Mr. Madison has been up to! Madison is hoping that the prestige of General Washington will convince the convention to at least consider the Virginia Plan.

Before we go into the library, let's drink in the stunning view. Gentle undulating hills of the Virginia piedmont spread out before us in a patchwork of green pastures dotted with the brown of freshly plowed fields. On the horizon, the hills give way to the mountains of Appalachia that invite us to dream of what lies over them. Here in the 18th Century, it's an era of romanticism. James Madison dreams of a nation that reaches over the mountains all the way to the Mississippi River, and George Washington from Mount Vernon, perched high on the banks of the Potomac, dreams of a network of rivers, lakes, and canals that stretch all the way to the Pacific. The Potomac dream is so popular it even has a name, "Potomac fever." America is a nation in its infancy. It is a time to dream and what Mr. Madison is working on is a dream built on a promise that never fails. Let's go inside now and get answers to our questions about the mirror into which 18th Century Americans peer, and learn what they regard as love.

We open the door to the library and are immediately struck by its simplicity. Montpelier is definitely not Monticello. Mr. Jefferson's library is elegant, impressive, and stocked with books from all over the world. Mr. Madison's library, while modest at this time, will grow over the decades to more than four thousand books. However in 1787, it's not the number of books in his library that matter. It is the kind that are important. The kind of books and documents that he has poured over the past months are important ones for they have given shape in his mind to an American republic.

Since we are visitors from the future, we know the type of republic that Mr. Madison envisioned. It is composed of two houses of Congress, the House of Representatives and the Senate. The President is the Commander-in-Chief and holds executive power. The court system, where a Supreme Court makes the final decision on all laws, is entirely separate. These three – Congress, the President, and the Supreme Court – check and balance one another. They share power to ensure that the government doesn't grab power that rightfully belongs to citizens. Our question is why? Why did the Virginia Plan call for this type of government? When we answer that question, we will know the mirror that 18th Century Americans held up and what they believed about love.

The first thing to know about late 18th Century America is that Mr. Madison and the other men that we now refer to as the Founding Fathers are Christians, and by today's lax standards, we would call them devout Christians. Professor Mark David Hall in his book, "Did America Have a Christian Founding?" stated that in 1776 all Americans "with the exception of two thousand Jews, identified himself or herself as a Christian. Approximately, 98 percent of them were Protestants, and the remaining 2 percent were Roman Catholic." (p. xxi) Professor Hall further notes that three-fourths of American Protestants were Calvinists. (Hall, p. 37) Catholics and Protestants alike acknowledge man's sinful nature, but Calvinists, who are by far the majority of Americans in this era believe that since the Fall of Adam, mankind is not simply prone to sin, but totally depraved and without hope except through the saving grace and love of Jesus Christ. Undoubtedly, 18th Century Americans looked to Christ as their Savior and model for life. They held up the mirror that reflects Christ's image of love, and while far from perfect, they sought to pattern their lives and this new form of self-government after what they saw in the mirror. What they saw is based on two tenants of faith: the total depravity of man and the total saving grace and love of Jesus Christ.

The old adage "Power corrupts and absolute power corrupts absolutely" likely didn't come into usage until the late 1800's. But, if the Calvinists in the late 1700's had heard it, they would totally agree with it. With this prevailing view of humanity, power within the central government had to be divided. No one man such as the President and no group of men such as Supreme Court justices or a few senators could be allowed to concentrate too much power. Mr. Madison believed that each branch of government would jealously guard their power and check any other branch that tried to usurp it. Plus, the citizens themselves were to provide a check on government power by voting out of office those who overstep the circumscribed powers of their office. Therefore, the mirror that Americans held up was Christ's mirror and it told them that they were very imperfect and in need of Christ's love. Mr. Madison and the delegates to the Philadelphia convention understood this point, and they were designing a government for a particular type of citizen.

With very few exceptions, America's Founding Fathers believed that self-government required a moral citizenry. In 1798, John Adams wrote that "our constitution was made only for a moral and religious people. It is wholly inadequate to the government of any other." A self-governing republic requires citizens with a strong sense of morality, because the government has limited powers. The real power resides with the citizens themselves, who police their own behavior, who follow the Ten

Commandments, and who believe that all are created in the image of God. In other words, the new American government needed citizens who are not easily angered, who are not proud, who do not envy their neighbor, and who delight in the truth. These are the characteristics of love that Paul described and they are hallmarks of a moral and law abiding citizenry.

At the Philadelphia convention that we now call the Constitutional Convention, the delegates recognized that Christ is the source of love and morality for the American people. Benjamin Franklin, the oldest delegate, proposed that each day's session be opened with prayer, and Roger Sherman, the second oldest delegate, seconded the proposal. It failed to pass, but God's involvement in the convention was noticed. Reflecting upon the Constitutional Convention, Mr. Madison in the Federalist Papers No. 37 wrote, "It is impossible, for the man of pious reflection, not to perceive in it a finger of that Almighty Hand... ." Professor Hall in his book, "Did America Have a Christian Founding?" notes that years after the convention, Franklin wrote, "the longer I live, the more convincing proofs I see of this truth – that God governs the affairs of men." (Hall, p. 4) Hall cites additional evidence of the Founding Fathers holding up Christ's mirror:

- John Marshall, the chief justice of the Supreme Court wrote that General Washington was "a sincere believer in the Christian faith, and a truly devout man." Further it was observed that "Every day of the year, he [Washington] rises at five in the morning; as soon as he is up, he dresses, then prays reverently to God." (Hall, p. 9)
- In his presidential Farewell Address, Washington wrote, "Of all the dispositions and habits which lead to political prosperity, religion and morality are indisputable supports." Later in his address, Washington notes

morality cannot "be maintained without religion." (Hall, p. 34) And, Christianity was the religion of America.

- Americans were so thoroughly Christian that Chief Justice Marshall in a keen observation believed that by simply looking at America's institutions, a person could guess that the citizens were Christian. He wrote, "It would be strange indeed, if with such a people, our institutions did not presuppose Christianity." (Hall, p. 31)

America's Founding Fathers created a self-government for a people who can govern themselves, because the citizens are holding up Christ's mirror and while the image is imperfect, they are striving to follow His pattern of perfect love. The relationship among perfect love, Christ, morality, and Christianity becomes evident by simply replacing "love" with "Jesus" in Paul's description of love.

Jesus is patient, Jesus is kind. He does not envy, he does not boast, he is not proud. He does not dishonor others, he is not self-seeking, he is not easily angered, he keeps no record of wrongs. Jesus does not delight in evil but rejoices with the truth. Jesus always protects, always trusts, always hopes, always perseveres. Jesus never fails.

The power of Christ's love shapes the way a person thinks. In Romans, Paul wrote, *Do not conform to the pattern of this world, but be transformed by the renewing of your mind. Then you will be able to test and approve what God's will is—his good, pleasing and perfect will.* (Romans 12:2) A citizenry with a renewed mind that does not conform to the pattern of this world, but is transformed by Christ's love is perhaps God's greatest blessing to America. And, the brilliance of the Founding Fathers was to create a republic that frees its moral citizens to create, to work, to worship, and to flourish as their renewed minds dictate. Americans are free to pick up any mirror they choose and gaze upon what it reflects. But, what happens to a people who no longer look in Christ's mirror? Jedidiah Morse, a Congregationalist pastor and the father of Samuel Morse, who invented the telegraph, in a 1799 sermon said, "All efforts to destroy the Foundation of our holy religion, ultimately tend to the subversion also of our political freedom and happiness. Whenever the pillars of Christianity shall be overthrown, our present republican form of government, and all the blessings which flow from them, must fall with them." (Hall, p. 33) Now, we must engage an unpleasant and even frightening question. What mirror do Americans hold up and look into today? It is certainly not Christ's mirror.

Today, Americans look into the same mirror held up by Adam and Eve at the Fall. It is the serpent's mirror that reflects man's desire to be god. Remember the serpent's words to Eve? *You will be like God.* (Genesis 3:5) The serpent's mirror tells American gods to be impatient, unkind, envious, boastful, proud, dishonorable, self-seeking, angry, hold grudges, delight in evil, and lie. All these sins, which are the opposite of love, are characteristics of people who believe they are gods. They don't see themselves as imperfect. Therefore, in their eyes, they are not sinful. If a person believes they are basically good and can perfect themselves, then why not perfect everything else? After all, they are gods, and that's what gods do. Therefore with the serpent's mirror in hand, American gods set out to control every aspect of life in order to perfect it according to the image they see.

They will control the climate and perfect it. Therefore, we must follow their prescription that calls for restricting and eventually eliminating fossil fuels. All the world's population will be poorer, but that's the price someone must pay for perfecting the climate. Those that hold the serpent's mirror have decided that they, not Nature, will assign gender. Therefore, they surgically and chemically alter children, change their birth names, and use different pronouns to perfect what Nature could not. American gods will decide what is true and what is false so they rewrite history, ban Shakespeare, and refuse to teach Western civilization in colleges and universities. They are merely perfecting education.

Those who gaze into the serpent's mirror say they can perfect public health. For two years, they locked schools and covered everyone's nose and mouth so that the youngest children's language development was harmed and older children were prevented from learning. It's just the price of perfecting public health we're told. However, the ultimate exercise of their god-like power is deciding when human life begins, and then choosing to end it whenever they desire. In this short list, we see poverty, famine, mutilation, propaganda, ignorance, and death. The greatest irony is that those that hold the serpent's mirror say they do these things out of love for the environment and people.

In 1943, C.S. Lewis, the Oxford and Cambridge scholar and Christian writer, foresaw a dystopian future similar to today. In a lecture entitled "The Abolition of Man," Lewis called, those who hold the serpent's mirror "man-moulders." He said, "They [the man-moulders] are not men at all: they are artifacts. Man's final conquest has proved to be the abolition of man," and "when all that says 'it is good' has been debunked, what says 'I want' remains." (Lewis, p. 64, 65) America's Founding Fathers were far from perfect men, and the American man-moulders who hold the serpent's mirror delight in pointing out their sin of slavery. They do this not to bring understanding of the human character, God, sin, and how people can get things wrong, as well as right. Rather, the sin of slavery is used to confuse and deceive us just as the serpent confused and deceived Adam and Eve. But, their deception is becoming less effective, because we can now see the future into which we are being led.

America's Founding Fathers led us into a land of goodness, promise, and hope, because they sought God's blessing and desired to hear God's proclamation, "It is good." American gods are leading us into a land of evil, lies, and despair, and just as Adam and Eve discovered their nakedness after rejecting God so too are Americans discovering our moral and spiritual nakedness. In their nakedness, American gods shout, "I want." And, what they want is control over every aspect of life and nature, because that's what gods want.

The wants of the American gods are the antithesis of the American way of life. Mr. Madison and the Founding Fathers gave us a government with limited powers to control and govern, because they relied upon a citizenry, whose minds are renewed by Christ's love, to control and govern themselves. With freedom to dream, to create, to work, to worship, and to prosper, Americans built a great nation that stretches from the Atlantic to the Pacific. This American dream is only possible because of a promise that never fails. The Bible calls promises "covenants" and God's never failing promise to those who love Christ is written in both the Old and New Testaments: *"This is the covenant I will make with them after that time, says the Lord. I will put my laws in their hearts, and I will write them on their minds."* (Jeremiah 31:33, Hebrews 10:16)

If God's laws are written in the hearts and minds of a nation's citizens, there is no need to write a multitude of laws to govern them. Mr. Madison knew this truth, but sadly few Americans know it today, which raises a frightening prospect that Americans are just now beginning to ponder. Adam and Eve looked in the serpent's mirror and lost Eden. Will we lose America? The answer is known only to God, but we do know this: only prayers of repentance, and petitions for the mercy, grace, and love of Christ can save us.

We have been in Mr. Madison's library for a long time and before leaving, we take one last look around. That the greatest governing document in the history of mankind was birthed in such a humble room is truly astonishing, but then we remember that Our Savior was birthed in a stable. We can only marvel at the ways in which God works. We have hope! With this thought in mind, we step onto Montpelier's front porch and look again at the mountains on the Western horizon. Let us dream again of an America that reflects the morals and goodness of Christ's love, and dedicate ourselves to the virtue of love.

Source: <u>Mark David Hall, Did America Have A Christian Founding? Separating Modern Myth From Historical Truth,</u> Published by Nelson Books of Thomas Nelson, 2019.

Chapter 6.
FORGIVENESS... the fragrance
of a godly nation

The gospel writer, Luke, provides an account of an uncomfortable scene at a dinner party hosted by a Pharisee named Simon. Jesus was a dinner guest, and when a woman, who perhaps had been a prostitute, crashed the party... well... let's allow Luke to tell the story.

36 When one of the Pharisees invited Jesus to have dinner with him, he went to the Pharisee's house and reclined at the table. 37 A woman in that town who lived a sinful life learned that Jesus was eating at the Pharisee's house, so she came there with an alabaster jar of perfume. 38 As she stood behind him at his feet weeping, she began to wet his feet with her tears. Then she wiped them with her hair, kissed them and poured perfume on them.

39 When the Pharisee who had invited him saw this, he said to himself, "If this man were a prophet, he would know who is touching him and what kind of woman she is—that she is a sinner."

40 Jesus answered him, "Simon, I have something to tell you."

"Tell me, teacher," he said.

41 "Two people owed money to a certain moneylender. One owed him five hundred denarii and the other fifty. 42 Neither of them had the money to pay him back, so he forgave the debts of both. Now which of them will love him more?"

43 Simon replied, "I suppose the one who had the bigger debt forgiven."

"You have judged correctly," Jesus said.

44 Then he turned toward the woman and said to Simon, "Do you see this woman? I came into your house. You did not give me any water for my feet, but she wet my feet with her tears and wiped them with her hair. ⁴⁵ You did not give me a kiss, but this woman, from the time I entered, has not stopped kissing my feet.⁴⁶ You did not put oil on my head, but she has poured perfume on my feet. ⁴⁷ Therefore, I tell you, her many sins have been forgiven—as her great love has shown. But whoever has been forgiven little loves little."

⁴⁸ Then Jesus said to her, "Your sins are forgiven."

⁴⁹ The other guests began to say among themselves, "Who is this who even forgives sins?"

⁵⁰ Jesus said to the woman, "Your faith has saved you; go in peace." (Luke 7:36-50)

In this story, Luke shows us three types of attitudes: a repentant heart, a hard heart, and the heart of Jesus, who forgave and redeemed the woman. Redemption is being accepted and allowed into the close presence of the person, who has been wronged. Sinners wrong God, and when Jesus allowed this woman, whose repentance was confirmed by her tears, close to him, he was painting a beautiful picture of redemption. In profound gratitude with a humble heart, she anointed Jesus' feet with perfume. As the fragrance filled the room even those seated far from Jesus and unaware of what was happening surely turned to identify the source of the delightful scent. What they saw was a tearful woman, but what they smelled was the sweet fragrance of forgiveness.

Simon's attitude, however, paints a very different picture. In his actions, we see a hard-hearted man, who was so convinced of his own righteousness that he could not see this woman as a person. All Simon saw was a deplorable sinner. In 1ˢᵗ Century Palestine, women were second-class citizens. That was one strike against her. She crashed his party – strike two – and she might have been a prostitute – strike three. We can almost imagine the disgusted look on Simon's face. Then, Luke tells us that Simon was not only judging the woman, he was judging Jesus too. How appallingly self-righteous!

The sharp contrast among Jesus, the woman, and Simon points to an important question about judging others. Why is it that God forgives and redeems sinners, but people will not? God, who is righteous, pure, holy, the Creator of all things, and holds divine power to judge, forgives and redeems. Man, who is sinful, given to all sorts of lust and vices, creates nothing that lasts – *the life of mortals is like grass* – and has no right to judge so very often refuses to forgive and is even less likely to redeem. It's quite a contrast! But, some people can and do forgive and redeem others. The woman forgiven and redeemed by Jesus is much more likely to be such a person; while Simon, who was so self-righteous that he judged the woman and Jesus, is likely to be a fault-finding, grudge-holding, unforgiving person. Not surprisingly, over the course of time, these two very different people produce very different outcomes in life with both reaping what they've sown.

Since this is true for individuals, can it also be true for nations? Is the outcome of a nation – its peace, prosperity, security, justice, and all the things that make for a good national life – dependent upon whether the citizens of that nation behave like Jesus or like Simon? Two true stories will answer this question. The first story will take us to Gettysburg, Pennsylvania in the year 1913, and in the second story, we will go Richmond, Virginia in the year 2020. In the first story, we will see the heart of the Jesus on display, and marvel at how the sweet fragrance of forgiveness softened battle-hardened hearts. In the second story, we will sadly see Simon's heart, and taste the bitter fruit of unforgiveness. Let's go now first to Gettysburg, Pennsylvania to witness the power of forgiveness.

* * *

The Gettysburg Battlefield, June 29 to July 4, 1913, the 50th anniversary of the battle

The anniversary event and battle reenactment spanned five days, and what days they were! Some remembered that each dawn was greeted by coos of mourning doves. They said the dove's haunting call seemed to ride the morning mist that rose from the land's gentle green pastures, giving the ethereal vapor a mystic voice as it twisted and turned, moved by an unseen hand until it disappeared, burned off by the heat of the rising sun. And, when dawn's grayness retreated, yielding to bright sunshine, the cardinal's song came. The showy red bird's sharp joyful trill filled the pastures and surrounding woods. Those who were there said it was as clear and pure, as any bird's song they'd ever heard. At least that was what they remembered, or did they only imagine it, because the songs of the cardinal and dove seemed for those few days to be speaking for the living and the dead of Gettysburg. For the living, the cardinal sang of forgiveness, redemption, and hope. For the dead, the soft coos of the dove riding the mist sang of remembrance – you are not forgotten, but we must move on from the pain and agony of war. Acceptance and moving on are part of the healing that comes from forgiveness and redemption.

Roughly 53,000 Civil War veterans participated in the 50th anniversary event, and they were all old men. But in 1863, they were young and full of fight. Counting both Union and Confederate troops, 157,289 men fought on the fields at Gettysburg, and the total casualties – the dead, wounded, and missing – were 51,112. Now, 50 years later, about 9,000 Rebels and 44,000 Yankees were back for a reenactment with a very different ending.

A large committee of veterans from both North and South had planned the event. During the five days, the veterans camped in tents that were provided by the U.S. government, who sponsored and funded this coming together. President Woodrow Wilson gave a 4th of July speech, but it wasn't the speeches, the military bands, or the waving of flags – both Stars & Stripes and Stars & Bars – that defined this anniversary. It was the veterans themselves. Grainy black and white photographs and silent movies document just how old they were. Most were in their 70's, a few were older, but at least one was in his early 60's. John Clem, who was nicknamed Johnny Shiloh, joined the US Army at age 10, as a drummer boy. He was just 12 years-old at the Gettysburg battle. Now, at age 62, he too was part of the old men contingent from both sides, who sang songs, told stories, marched with their units, and wore old uniforms or what was left of them. The highlight of the event was a reenactment of Pickett's Charge that today remains the subject of legend and myth written in blood.

On July 3, 1863 about 2 PM, 12,500 Confederates under the command of Major General George E. Pickett formed up to cross a large open expanse of farmland to attack the center of the Union line. The Union troops had the high ground. They were dug in atop a hill named Cemetery Ridge, and many were also shielded by a low stone wall. A frontal assault was understood to be dangerous and risky, but a heavy artillery barrage was delivered on the Union line to soften it up, and increase the odds of success. It did little. As Pickett's men advanced, they came under horrific rifle, musket, and canon fire. Twice, they came close to breaching the Union line at a point where the stone wall made a sharp turn. Each time they were repelled, and this spot became known as the "bloody angle." The shell-shocked and wounded, who were able to walk or crawl, retreated. During the retreat, General Lee encountered General Pickett along with a few wounded stragglers. Lee asked, "Where is your division?" Pickett responded, "General Lee, I have no division."

Now, 50 years later, this epic and legendary charge, which is a testament to the valor and courage of the men on both sides, was to be reenacted. The faded photos and grainy images from the silent movies are poignant. Old men with gray beards, some with canes, and others limping from old age and old wounds slowly made their way up Cemetery Ridge one last time. At the top of the hill behind the low stone wall stood the line of Union veterans, just as they had done that day a half-century ago. When the Confederates reached the wall, they shook hands, embraced, and wished each other well. This is forgiveness, and with forgiveness comes redemption.

Time had healed wounds of both the body and spirit. But, healing is not redemption. Healing means that you'll live, but it does not mean that you're alive. To be alive in the way God intends for us means that you are forgiven and redeemed, and in turn, you forgive and redeem those who have wronged you. After all, Our Lord taught us to pray, *Forgive us of our debts, as we forgive our debtors.* And, this is exactly what the old men on Cemetery Ridge were doing that day – forgiving and redeeming each other. Enemies no more, they were now American brothers, sharing a bond of suffering, forgiveness, and redemption. Are they so different than the woman at Jesus' feet? She had suffered. Forgiven and redeemed, she sat at the feet of Christ, accepted and loved. Forgiveness, like the perfume the woman poured on Jesus' feet, is the sweetest fragrance of life.

This 50th anniversary event revealed the character of America, and how Americans saw themselves in the early 20th Century. Little did the Gettysburg veterans know that America would soon need all the godly character that the Holy Spirit had bestowed upon the nation, because beginning the next year, 1914, the world was to be at war for most of the 20th Century. As we look back on the 20th Century, we see that our peace, prosperity, and security very much depended on America's character. A character of valor and courage to win two world wars, and a character of forgiveness and redemption to make our former enemies, Germany and Japan, our allies. We were a nation under God, and blessed by God. Nations, like individuals, do reap what they sow. In Gettysburg and during the 20th Century wars, we see evidence of the woman's story of forgiveness and redemption in America. Now it's time to tell the American version of Simon's story, and taste the bitter fruit of it. Let's go now to Richmond, Virginia.

* * *

On the banks of the James River, Richmond, Virginia, summer 2020.

History rides the currents of the James River. Downstream from Richmond is Jamestown where America began, close by is Williamsburg where America's spirit of freedom took shape, and just a bit further away on the York River is Yorktown where America's freedom was won. At Richmond, high on the river's north bank, where we are standing, 175 years of history rests in the soil of Hollywood Cemetery. Two U.S. presidents – James Monroe and John Tyler – are buried here, as is Jefferson Davis, the president of the Confederate States. Two Supreme Court Justices, six Virginia governors, a host of senators, congressmen, judges, generals, several tobacco barons, and a smattering of historians, writers, and college presidents among others all rest eternally within the gates of Hollywood Cemetery. General George Pickett is one of Hollywood's generals, and now we have a connection to Gettysburg. But, Pickett's grave is not why we're here. What we seek is tucked away in a corner of the cemetery and it's most unusual.

In Hollywood's northwest corner is a pyramid of stacked granite stones that rises to a height of 90 feet. The four faces of the pyramid perfectly taper and slope to the pinnacle, which is a remarkable feat of craftsmanship considering that the granite is rough-hewn blocks. Achieving such clean lines and precise angles of the pyramid, when each block is uniquely shaped, is a lasting testament to the talent of the masons who laid them. Perhaps, the uniqueness of the individual blocks amassed for a common purpose is reflective of the lives of the 18,000 Confederates who are buried nearby. Individually they answered Virginia's call, and now they collectively rest here at Hollywood Cemetery's Monument to the Confederate War Dead.

The loss of life the in the Civil War was staggering. Over 31,000 Virginians died. By comparison, about 11,000 Virginians died in World War II at a time when the state's population was much larger than it was in the 1860's. No family was left untouched, and after the Civil War, a campaign to bring Virginia's fallen sons home from far-flung battlefields was launched. Once in Richmond, they would be given a proper burial, and to honor the dead, a Hollywood Cemetery women's organization raised the funds and commissioned building the monument that was dedicated in 1869. What was happening in Richmond was also occurring across the South. Women's organizations formed to locate Confederate war dead, return them home, and give them a proper burial. This reinternment effort was part of a larger post-war Southern movement that is called the Lost Cause.

Today, historians debate the value and merits of the Lost Cause, and the movement is often disparaged, as an attempt to cover-up facts and harsh realities of the Civil War. The Lost Cause minimized the fact that African slavery was a compelling moral reason for the war, and the movement romanticized the valor and virtues of the South in comparison to the North. A harsher interpretation of the Lost Cause is that it justified Jim Crow laws and segregation of African Americans. One aspect of the Lost Cause, however, is not debated. It was an effort to heal from the war that had completely destroyed the South, and robbed families of fathers, husbands, brothers, and sons. In 1865,

Reconstruction did not include anything similar to the Marshall Plan that rebuilt Europe after World War II. Any virtue of forgiveness that was present in the North at the end of the Civil War died in the aftermath of President Lincoln's assassination. The South was defeated and occupied by Federal troops. In this environment, the Lost Cause was born.

As part of the Lost Cause, throughout the South but especially in Richmond, statues were erected to Confederate heroes. On May 29, 1890, an impressive towering statue of General Lee on horseback was unveiled in Richmond. Over the next several years, lesser, but still large and artful monuments to Generals "Stonewall" Jackson, and JEB Stuart, along with a statue to Jefferson Davis were placed on a wide boulevard flanking the Lee statue. The final Confederate monument added was to Matthew Fontaine Maury, who resigned his commission in the U.S. Navy to serve in the Confederate Navy primarily as their envoy to Great Britain. Maury's place on the boulevard, however, was more in recognition of his contributions to science than to his wartime service. Maury was a world renown oceanographer, meteorologist, and physical geographer. The fact that Maury was part of this pantheon of Confederate heroes illustrates that victories and wartime accomplishments weren't the sole criteria for a monument. Character mattered, and these were men of character, who endured hardship and suffered yet persevered. With completion of the monuments, trees were planted, and as the 1890's gave way to the 1900's, impressive gas lit townhomes were built on the street that was named Monument Avenue.

As the decades passed, art festivals were held on the boulevard under the shade trees, and each Easter Sunday, Monument Avenue was turned into a pedestrian mall, where friends and families strolled the lovely street in their Sunday finest. By the late 20th Century, Monument Avenue hosted one of the nation's largest 10K runs. Tens of thousands of runners passed by the monuments on their way to the finish line. The only thought, if any, given to the monuments was that they were public art – beautiful statues on a lovely street lined with handsome townhomes. The Civil War to most everyone was nothing more than another chapter in a high school history book. The Lost Cause was not even that – only history buffs were even aware of it. The monuments, while part of a past that was mostly forgotten, were to Richmonders what the Arc de Triomphe is to Parisians or Trafalgar Square is to Londoners. But, in the 21st Century, 130 years after they were gifted to the city, the monuments over a period of months were defaced, destroyed, chopped up, and carted off to a waste processing facility. General Lee and the others were victims of rioters in the summer of 2020.

Here we see the American version of Simon, who was unwilling to forgive, and judging with a harshness that prevented him from seeing an individual as a person. Simon, the Pharisee, offered no forgiveness and certainly no redemption, and neither did the "Simons," in 2020, who destroyed Richmond's monuments, as well as monuments all across America, including those of George Washington, Thomas Jefferson, and Christopher Columbus. Jesus asked Simon, *"Do you see this woman?* No, he could not see her as a person. He only saw a sinner, a prostitute, and anyone who thought otherwise received his harsh judgment. Likewise, the 2020 "Simons" could not see the people of more than a century ago, who struggled to find some dignity and meaning in what they had suffered and endured, and in their struggle to reconcile the pain and loss of the war, they honored Virginians of virtue and courage, because they had nothing else to honor and no other place to put the pain of their sin. And so it was too with the sinful woman, who crashed Simon's dinner party.

First, she wept and washed Jesus' feet with her tears, then she poured out perfume from the alabaster jar. Before Christ's forgiveness, she had no place to put the pain of her sins. Perhaps, metaphorically she placed her pain in the alabaster jar, and with forgiveness, her pain was transformed into a beautiful fragrance. You see, this woman was forgiven before she came to Simon's dinner party. Jesus said, *I tell you, her many sins have been forgiven.* He did not say *are forgiven.* Christ had forgiven her sometime before the dinner party, and she came to thank him in this very public way. What she poured out on his feet was the pain of past sins that with forgiveness were transformed into a beautiful fragrance for all to enjoy. So it was with Richmonders over a century ago.

They paid a heavy price for their sins, and in their pain, they wept and searched for a place to put their heartache. Their alabaster jar was Monument Avenue, and in it the pain of their sins was transformed into graceful statues that – like the woman's perfume – were purchased at great cost given as donations. Not all at once, but over time, these very public statues did help heal, and with time forgiveness came. We saw it in Gettysburg on the 50th anniversary of the battle. It wasn't perfect forgiveness; only Jesus offers that. But in our imperfect ways, Americans after the Civil War did forgive, and this is uniquely American because other nations divided in a civil war often harbor bitterness for a century or more. But, not Americans! We believe, or perhaps we once believed, that forgiveness is a virtue.

What the "Simons" of 2020 did can only be grasped by returning to Simon's dinner party and writing a different ending. Imagine that as the woman was washing Jesus' feet with her tears, Simon came over, grabbed the alabaster jar, and smashed it on the floor. The perfume's wonderful fragrance would still have filled the room, because it is Christ, who forgives and transforms pain into beauty. But, Simon's destructive action would be saying to everyone in the room that he had no use for Christ's forgiveness. In taking something that wasn't his to take and destroying it, Simon – if he had actually done it – would be rejecting healing, rejecting forgiveness, and rejecting redemption. In place of these good and noble sentiments, he would be fomenting anger and hatred. This is exactly what the "Simons" of 2020 did.

In the actual biblical account, Jesus *turned toward the woman and said to Simon, "Do you see this woman?* Today, Jesus is asking Americans a corresponding question, Americans, do you see yourselves? What is the national spirit that we desire? Is it a spirit of forgiveness, where former enemies embrace? Or is it a spirit of vengeance, where things of beauty lie broken? Forgiveness is the fragrance of a godly nation, and at this time in our history, as was done after the Civil War, we must lavishly practice this virtue, forgiving even the "Simons" of 2020, because that is what Christ requires of us. When Americans, like the old men of Gettysburg, forgive, our nation again will be filled with the most heavenly of fragrances, the scent of forgiveness.

Chapter 7.
COURAGE... to know truth and change.

[28] *"Lord, if it's you,"* Peter replied, *"tell me to come to you on the water."*

[29] *"Come,"* he said.

Then Peter got down out of the boat, walked on the water and came toward Jesus. *[30]* *But when he saw the wind, he was afraid and, beginning to sink, cried out, "Lord, save me!"*

[31] *Immediately Jesus reached out his hand and caught him. "You of little faith,"* he said, *"why did you doubt?"* (Mathew 14:28-31)

Was it only faith that Peter lacked, or did he also lack courage? Earlier that day on the shore by the Sea of Galilee, Jesus fed five thousand with five small barley loaves and two small fish. (Matthew 14:9) Peter witnessed this miracle. Surely, it strengthened his faith that Jesus is indeed the Messiah, the Anointed One, the Son of God. Later that evening, the disciples were rowing across the Sea of Galilee, but Jesus remained on shore. When they were about three or four miles from shore, a storm whipped up the wind and waves. Peter and the other disciples, several who were experienced fishermen, certainly knew the danger of a nighttime storm. Stay in the boat, bail it, and row through the waves. But, then Jesus appeared in the darkness, walking calmly over the waves, and Matthew records that Peter broke the cardinal rule of the sea. He by faith got out of the boat to join Jesus on the water. He too was standing atop the turbulent water, but then his courage failed. When courage flees, faith hides, and Peter began to sink. In that moment of darkness, fear, and despair, Jesus saved Peter. Matthew tells us that *Jesus reached out his hand and caught him.*

There are moments in our lives and in the life of nations where we must choose between courageously knowing truth or cowardly abandoning truth in exchange for perceived safety. Courage or cowardice that is the choice. In the storm of life, will we be like Peter, who had the courage to believe the truth of Christ, and therefore, climb out of the boat and experience – however brief – the miracle of walking on water? Or, will we be like the other eleven disciples, who cowered in the flimsy safety of a storm tossed boat and never experienced the miraculous? Amazingly, in 1775 this was precisely the choice that America's thirteen colonies faced. King George III's parliament hurled a storm of laws and draconian taxes at the colonies, and then dispatched soldiers to ensure compliance. Courage or cowardice? Remain seated in Great Britain's ship of state and live as a slave to the king? Or, climb out of the boat to either freedom or death? Truth, courage, and freedom or lies, cowardice, and slavery – that was the choice.

We're going to meet a man who put this choice to the colonies. He was a man of faith, integrity, and character, whose brilliant words gave clarity of thought, set hearts on fire, and forged backbones of iron. Let's go now to colonial Virginia and meet this remarkable man.

* * *

St. John's Church, Richmond, the Virginia Colony, March 21 – 27, 1775

The view from the churchyard is stunning. St. John's Church sits atop a commanding hill that is aptly named Church Hill, and spread out in every direction is the gentle Virginia countryside that is just beginning to awaken from its winter slumber. Through these elysian fields, the James River flows first violently and then peacefully. Richmond sits at the river's fall line. Upriver from the city, rapids churn, but below it, the ferocity of the river melts into the gentleness of Tidewater Virginia. At Richmond, the river makes a decision to change how it conducts itself, and that same decision will be made this week in Richmond for the entire Virginia Colony. These are turbulent times for the thirteen colonies. Change is surely coming. How shall Virginia conduct herself? It will be debated and then put to a vote. Normally, legislative matters are addressed in the House of Burgesses in Williamsburg, but the royal governor, John Murray, his lordship, the Earl of Dunmore, dismissed the House and has refused to reconvene it by order of the British crown.

For ten years, the colonies have endured London's punitive, harsh, and unfair treatment. The 1765 Stamp Act that put a tax on all paper documents is hated. A little over a year ago in December 1773, the Sons of Liberty threw an entire shipment of tea overboard into Boston Harbor. Back in London, Parliament decided that the Massachusetts Colony needed to be taught a lesson. Four draconian laws aimed at punishing the colony were passed, and one of those laws allowed British soldiers to be quartered in private homes at the expense of the homeowner. These laws quickly became known as the Intolerable Acts, and they produced only more dissent and anger. A little over six months ago in September 1774, the colonies convened the First Continental Congress in Philadelphia. Now, a second meeting of that congress is to be held, and this gathering in Richmond, called the Second Virginia Convention, is to elect delegates to represent the colony at the Second Continental Congress.

Selecting delegates is perhaps the least controversial topic. The real issue before this Virginia convention is whether or not to prepare for war. Fairfax County in northern Virginia has already commissioned a militia, and counties throughout the colonies are forming militias. Is Virginia to be on the path of war, independence, and liberty? Britain's army and navy are the most powerful military forces in the world, and victory over them is as an unlikely as walking on water. Or, is Virginia to remain subservient to the royal governor in Williamsburg and accept the so-called peace that comes from acquiescence? The James River at Richmond chooses either the turbulence of rapids or the peace of Tidewater, and that is the choice that Virginia must also make at Richmond. Will Virginians make war for liberty or settle for peace as slaves? Will Virginia be brave like Peter and step out of the boat, or will she be like the other eleven, who cowered and hoped to ride out the storm? The mood of the 120 delegates assembled in the sanctuary of St. John's Church is hard to read, but the sentiment seemed to favor staying in the boat and hoping for the best. At least that seemed the sentiment until the delegate from Hanover County rose to speak. His name? Patrick Henry.

"No man thinks more highly than I do of the patriotism, as well as abilities, of the very worthy gentlemen who have just addressed the House. But different men often see the same subject in different lights; and, therefore, I hope it will not be thought disrespectful to those gentlemen if, entertaining as I do opinions of a character very opposite to theirs, I shall speak forth my sentiments freely and without reserve. This is no time for ceremony. The questing before the House is one of awful moment to this country. For my own part, I consider it as nothing less than a question of freedom or slavery; and in proportion to the magnitude of the subject ought to be the freedom of the debate. It is only in this way that we can hope to arrive at truth, and fulfill the great responsibility which we hold to God and our country. Should I keep back my opinions at such a time, through fear of giving offense, I should consider myself as guilty of treason towards my country, and of an act of disloyalty toward the Majesty of Heaven, which I revere above all earthly kings.

"Mr. President, it is natural for man to indulge in the illusions of hope. We are apt to shut our eyes against a painful truth, and listen to the song of that siren till she transforms us into beasts.

Is this the part of wise men, engaged in a great and arduous struggle for liberty? Are we disposed to be of the number of those who, having eyes, see not, and, having ears, hear not, the things which so nearly concern their temporal salvation? For my part, whatever anguish of spirit it may cost, I am willing to know the whole truth; to know the worst, and to provide for it. I have but one lamp by which my feet are guided, and that is the lamp of experience. I know of no way of judging the future but by the past. And judging by the past, I wish to know what there has been in the conduct of the British ministry for the last ten years to justify those hopes with which gentlemen have been pleased to solace themselves and the House. Is it that insidious smile with which our petition has been lately received? Trust it not, sir; it will prove a snare to your feet. Suffer not yourselves to be betrayed with a kiss. Ask yourselves how this gracious reception of our petition comports with those warlike preparations which cover our waters and darken our land. Are fleets and armies necessary to a work of love and reconciliation? Have we shown ourselves so unwilling to be reconciled that force must be called in to win back our love? Let us not deceive ourselves, sir. These are the implements of war and subjugation; the last arguments to which kings resort. I ask gentlemen, sir, what means this martial array, if its purpose be not to force us to submission? Can gentlemen assign any other possible motive for it? Has Great Britain any enemy, in this quarter of the world, to call for all this accumulation of navies and armies? No, sir, she has none. They are meant for us: they can be meant for no other.

"They are sent over to bind and rivet upon us those chains which the British ministry have been so long forging. And what have we to oppose to them? Shall we try argument? Sir, we have been trying that for the last ten years. Have we anything new to offer upon the subject? Nothing. We have held the subject up in every light of which it is capable; but it has been all in vain. Shall we resort to entreaty and humble supplication? What terms shall we find which have not been already exhausted? Let us not, I beseech you, sir, deceive ourselves. Sir, we have done everything that could be done to avert the storm which is now coming on.

"We have petitioned; we have remonstrated; we have supplicated; we have prostrated ourselves before the throne, and have implored its interposition to arrest the tyrannical hands of the ministry and Parliament. Our petitions have been slighted; our remonstrances have produced additional violence and insult; our supplications have been disregarded; and we have been spurned, with contempt, from the foot of the throne! In vain, after these things, may we indulge the fond hope of peace and reconciliation. There is no longer any room for hope. If we wish to be free– if we mean to preserve inviolate those inestimable privileges for which we have been so long contending–if we mean not basely to abandon the noble struggle in which we have been so long engaged, and which we have pledged ourselves never to abandon until the glorious object of our contest shall be obtained–we must fight! I repeat it, sir, we must fight! An appeal to arms and to the God of hosts is all that is left us!

"They tell us, sir, that we are weak; unable to cope with so formidable an adversary. But when shall we be stronger? Will it be the next week, or the next year? Will it be when we are totally disarmed, and when a British guard shall be stationed in every house? Shall we gather strength by irresolution and inaction? Shall we acquire the means of effectual resistance by lying supinely on our backs and hugging the delusive phantom of hope, until our enemies shall have bound us hand and foot? Sir, we are not weak if we make a proper use of those means which the God of nature hath placed in our power. The millions of people, armed in the holy cause of liberty, and in such a country as that which we possess, are invincible by any force which our enemy can send against us. Besides, sir, we shall not fight our battles alone.

There is a just God who presides over the destinies of nations, and who will raise up friends to fight our battles for us. The battle, sir, is not to the strong alone; it is to the vigilant, the active, the brave. Besides, sir, we have no election. If we were base enough to desire it, it is now too late to retire from the contest. There is no retreat but in submission and slavery! Our chains are forged! Their clanking may be heard on the plains of Boston! The war is inevitable–and let it come! I repeat it, sir, let it come.

"It is in vain, sir, to extenuate the matter. Gentlemen may cry, Peace, Peace– but there is no peace. The war is actually begun! The next gale that sweeps from the north will bring to our ears the clash of resounding arms! Our brethren are already in the field! Why stand we here idle? What is it that gentlemen wish? What would they have? Is life so dear, or peace so sweet, as to be purchased at the price of chains and slavery? Forbid it, Almighty God! I know not what course others may take; but as for me, give me liberty or give me death!"

Courage is like the wind. You can't see it. You can't grasp it. It suddenly appears and you feel its effects. But, unlike the wind which is common, courage is rare and when it appears it is not gentle or subtle like a breeze. Courage has the force of a tornado. With courage Peter walked on water, and with courage, Patrick Henry moved, not just the Virginia Colony but, the entire world to a new plane of liberty and human dignity.

Death was the punishment for treason against the crown. As they met in Richmond, the royal governor in Williamsburg was readying his troops to root-out these traitors. Meanwhile in St. John's Church, Henry's words were reasoned, truthful, courageous, and eloquent, but what he was really imploring the gentlemen from Virginia to do was put their necks into the noose that King George III was preparing for them. By voting yea, on a resolution proposed by Henry, they were putting the noose around their necks. The resolution read:

"Resolved therefore that this Colony be immediately put into a posture of Defence," that a Committee be appointed "to prepare a Plan for embodying, arming, and disciplining such a Number of Men as may be sufficient for that purpose."

Henry's speech carried the day, giving just enough men the courage to vote yea. The resolution narrowly passed by a vote of 65 to 60. At Richmond, the Virginia colony, like the James River, changed its conduct. It would henceforth be on a path toward war, and less than one month later war came. On the night of April 18th, Paul Revere made his famous ride, and as dawn broke on the next morning, America was at war. The Battle of Lexington and Concord was underway and with it came the Revolutionary War. Across the colonies, "Give me liberty or give me death!" became the rallying cry.

Today, St. John's Church still sits atop Church Hill in Richmond. The view is still magnificent, the James River still churns and then abruptly meanders into tidewater, and each Sunday afternoon during the summer months, Patrick Henry's "Give me liberty or give me death" speech is reenacted in the church sanctuary. Down river in Williamsburg, the colonial town has been reconstructed, and in the town's green common, redcoat troops still muster and march to the delight of tourists. At Williamsburg, the fury of the rapids is long spent. The river is broad and peaceful, and from it gentle breezes refresh summer tourists. It's so easy and comforting to think that this bucolic scene is America itself. That enemies of liberty have all been vanquished in 20th Century wars, and that courage to confront enemies of truth and liberty is only something you read about; a quaint virtue from the past that is no longer needed. Yet, it is at this moment of stupor and dullness that courage is needed the most.

The courage to speak truth, when no one wishes to hear truth. The courage to live a life of virtue in a time moral depravity. The courage to live free, while being attacked, cancelled, and censored. History teaches that the enemies of truth and liberty are never truly vanquished. They can be defeated in battles, and they can suffer setbacks, but they never stop their war, because it is a war that began in the human heart, when Adam and Eve believed they could be gods. Throughout the centuries from Eden until today in the 21st Century, the enemies of truth and liberty all carry the same conviction: they know better, they are superior, and they are enlightened. They sing the siren song of every tyrant – believe my lies, surrender your liberty, give me power, and I will usher you into a utopia, because I am god. Yet, the heaven these tyrant gods create in the end turns out to be hell.

King George III and Parliament told Americans that the taxes were for their own good. They said that London's commandeering of colonial government under the Intolerable Acts was only for better governance, and when they stationed redcoats in cities, tracked everyone's movements, and filled America's harbors with British warships, they said it was to protect Americans, to make sure everyone is safe, and to ensure equity. In his speech, one by one, Patrick Henry stripped away these lies, and forced comfortable men, wealthy men, well-connected men, who were leaders in their communities to face the truth that an oppressive force had invaded America. Then, Henry articulated the choice that was theirs: "Why stand we here idle? What is it that gentlemen wish? What would they have? Is life so dear, or peace so sweet, as to be purchased at the price of chains and slavery? Forbid it, Almighty God!"

Has not an oppressive force invaded America today? And, what about comfortable Americans, affluent Americans, well-connected Americans, who are leaders in business, education, churches, foundations, and government, do they wish to hear the truth about America's crisis? Look at our cities! Are they not Exhibit A in God's court that enemies of light, goodness, morality, truth, and liberty have invaded America's cities? King George III had limited power. He could post troops in town squares, station them in government offices, and quarter them in a few homes. Their bright red coats always identified who they were. But, one thing they could not do is influence, pervert, control, and manipulate the hearts and minds of millions of Americans as is possible today. Americans today are like the delegates at the Second Virginia Convention, who – until Patrick Henry spoke – preferred to hope that it all goes away and America will return to normal. In 1775, the redcoat army was not simply going to go away, and neither will today's enemies of truth of liberty. Therefore, let's look more closely at Henry's speech to see if what moved the comfortable and powerful gentlemen of Virginia two centuries ago might yet again move sedentary and affluent Americans today.

Henry's words had remarkable power, because they carried courage to the heart, truth to the mind, and humility to the soul. He began with humility saying, "different men often see the same subject in different lights; and, therefore, I hope it will not be thought disrespectful to those gentlemen if, entertaining as I do opinions of a character very opposite to theirs, I shall speak forth my sentiments freely and without reserve. This is no time for ceremony." Sadly, such respect for opinions different from our own is a rarity today. Throughout American history, it's not unusual for politicians to ridicule and demean their opponents; after all they want to win. But, after the race is over, political opponents came together to govern, which means they entertained ideas that are opposite to their own and reached compromises. Today, the ridicule and demeaning of those who hold opposite opinions and views never stops and it is not limited to politics. Universities enforce a strict orthodoxy that allows no dissent. Surprisingly, today's so-called science is the same. Question climate change, vaccines, gender fluidity, or a host of other dogmas that are "settled science" and you will be shouted down, shutdown, and cancelled. Where is humility? Humble people respect others, but humility in America is gone, and freedom of speech, expression, and thought left with it. If America in the 21ˢᵗ Century is to be a nation of truth and liberty, we first must be a nation that is humble, respectful, and kind, like Patrick Henry was to those who disagreed with him.

After speaking humility to the soul, Henry spoke truth to the mind. He said, "Let us not, I beseech you, sir, deceive ourselves. Sir, we have done everything that could be done to avert the storm which is now coming on. We have petitioned; we have remonstrated; we have supplicated; we have prostrated ourselves before the throne, and have implored its interposition to arrest the tyrannical hands of the ministry and Parliament. Our petitions have been slighted; our remonstrances have produced additional violence and insult; our supplications have been disregarded; and we have been spurned, with contempt, from the foot of the throne! In vain, after these things, may we indulge the fond hope of peace and reconciliation. There is no longer any room for hope." This was the truth of America's situation in 1775. What is the truth of America's situation today? It is time for men and women of good and honest character to address this question truthfully, and to do so requires courage.

At St. John's Church, Henry spoke courage to the heart. He was known throughout Virginia for his eloquence and his ability to stir hearts. This reputation was won mainly in the courtroom. Henry was a lawyer, who won seemingly unwinnable cases with the power of his words. It's one thing to be moved by words and settle a civil lawsuit in favor of Henry's client, and quite another to stick one's neck in the hangman's noose. Therefore, what was the power behind his words? He humbly spoke truth, but there is more. Through his words, he freely shared the hope and confidence that was in his heart with the delegates. He said, "Sir, we are not weak if we make a proper use of those means which the God of nature hath placed in our power. The millions of people, armed in the holy cause of liberty, and in such a country as that which we possess, are invincible by any force which our enemy can send against us. Besides, sir, we shall not fight our battles alone. There is a just God who presides over the destinies of nations, and who will raise up friends to fight our battles for us. The battle, sir, is not to the strong alone; it is to the vigilant, the active, the brave." The power of Patrick Henry's words that day was "a just God who presides over the destinies of nations."

God does not change. He *is the same yesterday and today and forever.* (Hebrews 13:8) The just God, who gave courage to 65 delegates at the Second Virginia Convention to vote for liberty even if it meant death, still reigns in heaven and on earth. When America once again calls upon His Name, humility and truth will return to the land, and when these virtues have transformed our souls and minds, then God will send courage to our hearts. And, "millions of people, armed in the holy cause of liberty, and in such a country as that which we possess, are invincible by any force which our enemy can send against us."

In the storm, Peter trusted Jesus and found the courage to climb out of the boat. Yes, he sank, but he also walked on water and Jesus rescued him. Peter experienced the miraculous. In storm tossed America today, let us have the courage of Peter and Patrick Henry. Let us have the courage to trust God, climb out of the boat in this storm, and courageously stand "in the holy cause of liberty." At Richmond in 1775, Virginia found the courage to know truth and change. Will we?

Chapter 8.
HONOR... at a time that try men's soul

Honor. It's rarely thought of, but routinely mentioned.

When a judge enters his courtroom: "All raise for the Honorable...."

When a Member of Congress is formally addressed: "The Honorable..."

At a banquet: "The guest of honor is..."

In high school: "The National Honor Society selects..."

When we meet a famous or noteworthy person: "It's an honor to meet you..."

In golf the privilege of teeing off first: "You have the honor..."

At a retirement party: "It's been an honor to work with you..."

Yet in today's world of presumed familiarity and exaggerated informality, actually honoring someone, whether it's parents, your boss, your spouse, your doctor, or the stranger on the street, is not expected. With little to no expectation of honor, we've lost something much more valuable than manners and civility. We've lost a characteristic that tells us about God and ourselves.

Honor runs throughout the Bible. In the New International Version, honor is mentioned 211 times. Many of these references involve honoring a king or important person, a practice that has continued from antiquity until the present. However, in Exodus we get a clue that honor entails something more than a cultural protocol when we read the fifth commandment. *"Honor your father and your mother, so that you may live long in the 'and the Lord your God is giving you."* (Exodus 20:12) The commandment doesn't say "obey your father and mother," nor does it say "appreciate," "cherish," or "look up to" them. We are to honor our parents. Therefore, the parent-child relationship, one of the two deepest and most intimate of human relationships – marriage is the other one – involves honor at its core. Why? For that clue, we have to go to the last book of the Bible, the Book of Revelation.

In the fourth chapter, we read:

> *"You are worthy, our Lord and God,*
> *to receive glory and honor and power,*
> *for you created all things,*
> *and by your will they were created*
> *and have their being."* (Revelation 4:11)

These words are spoken by the twenty-four elders, who surround the throne of God. However, before saying these words, they lay their crowns before the throne and prostrate themselves in worship of the Living God, who is worthy *to receive glory and honor and power*. This eternal heavenly praise indicates that honor, along with glory and power, are intrinsic to God and creation. Artists, who create great works, whether it's a painting or music or some other medium, express their character in their art. If the character of mortal artists is present in their art, then certainly the character of the Eternal God is present in his creation. Therefore, honor plus glory and power are evident in creation itself.

David in his psalms confirms that honor is inherent to the Creator – creature relationship. In Psalm 8, he wrote:

> [W]*hat is mankind that you are mindful of them,*
> *human beings that you care for them?*
> [5] *You have made them a little lower than the angel*
> *and crowned them with glory and honor.*
> (Psalm 8:4-5)

God has crowned us with two of the three attributes for which he is praised in heaven. Because we are created in God's image, by birthright, God has bestowed us with honor, and as the Bible teaches, we are to honor others, who too are created in God's image. Sadly, we spend our lives either unaware or not caring about honor that comes from God, and as a result, we dishonor ourselves and treat others dishonorably. Worse, we often honor what is vile, and behave exactly the opposite of how God intended. David mentioned this evil aspect of humanity in a psalm. He tells us that the wicked *freely strut about when what is vile is honored by the human race.* (Psalm 12:8)

Surely, there are consequences associated with what we honor and dishonor. We are commanded to honor our father and mother *so that you may live long in the land the Lord your God is giving you.* (Psalm 12:8) Does that mean, if you don't honor your parents, dishonor others, and honor vileness, your time in the land, i.e., your life, will be shortened? And that perhaps, due to lack of honor you could lose your home and everything that you've worked for? Is what you honor and dishonor really that important? To answer these questions, we are going back in time to the year 1776. After an initial success in Boston, General Washington and the Continental Army are fighting a British invasion of New York City. The situation is dire. Yet in this dark hour we will witness an amazing display of honor that reveals the character of a man who shaped our nation. Let's go now to New Jersey.

* * *

Somewhere near Hackensack, New Jersey, November 22, 1776

"These are the times that try men's souls. The summer soldier and sunshine patriot will, in this crisis, shrink from the service of their country; but he that stands it now, deserves the love and thanks of man and woman."

Thomas Paine, the author of the widely read pamphlet, *Common Sense*, that had so galvanized liberty-loving Americans in 1775, wrote the above lines in response to the suffering and hardship of the Continental Army. In the autumn of 1776, the army was in full retreat. Many men had no shoes. Most wore only rags and some were shirtless. All were hungry. Worse, an unrelenting cold November rain chilled the body and the soul. Paine, a civilian aide to General Nathanael Greene, was an eye witness to the army's misery, and he published his account in a pamphlet entitled, *Crisis*. But, rather than detailing the desperate conditions, Paine, an unflagging patriot, ennobled the suffering and in the process penned a line that is quoted to this day, "These are the times that try men's souls." The trying times were events that had unfolded in New York over the previous three months.

Under General Washington's command, the Continental Army spent the summer of 1776 digging-in and fortifying New York. With the British army's withdrawal from Boston in March, the Americans were certain the British would turn their attention to New York, and they did. On July 2, just two days before the Declaration of Independence was signed in Philadelphia, an armada of 120 British warships sailed into New York harbor carrying over 30,000 troops under the command of General William Howe. Headquarters were established on Staten Island, and the British command began their campaign to defeat these upstart Americans and end this rebellion against King George III.

On August 22, General Howe landed 22,000 British and Hessian troops on Long Island. Outnumbered two-to-one, the Continental Army engaged the British. As the battle ensued, they were in danger of having their line broken and being overrun. Washington had little choice but to retreat to Brooklyn Heights. During the night, thanks to wind and rain that hid their movements, the Continental Army was able to cross the East River and escape to Manhattan. On September 9th, Washington convened a war council and the decision was made to evacuate Lower Manhattan. Throughout September, the British pushed the Continental Army farther and farther up the island of Manhattan.

British warships sailed up the Hudson River and bombarded the already outnumbered Americans with cannon fire.

Fort Lee on the New Jersey bank of the Hudson River, and Fort Washington opposite it on the New York side were designed to sink any British Man-of-War that attempted to run their gauntlet. Plus, the river between the forts was littered with supposedly hull-crushing obstacles. But, the British sailed right past the forts with little problem. With almost unimpeded navigation of the Hudson, the Continental Army's escape route across the river was in danger of being cut-off, leaving them trapped on Manhattan Island. Washington again had no choice, but to retreat across the Hudson into New Jersey. To guard their withdrawal, he left troops on the New York side of the river under the command of General Charles Henry Lee.

General Lee was an unusual American officer. He was British trained, and an experienced combat veteran, having served in the Seven Years War. After the war, he resigned his commission in the British army, and took a position in the Polish army. After that service, he bought an estate and settled in Virginia. His European training and broad experience had made him a contender to be named Commander-in-Chief of the Continental Army, but Congress selected Washington instead. In keeping with his character, Washington accepted and trusted Lee, even though he was a competitor and an openly ambitious man. In recognition of Lee's service and accomplishments, Washington named the fort on the New Jersey side of the Hudson River in his honor. But, such honors were far from Washington's mind now. To save his army, he had to move them – horses, cannons, tents, supplies, everything – across the Hudson. With plans for the retreat laid, Washington ordered General Lee and his troops to position themselves in Manhattan just north of the evacuation point to guard the retreat into New Jersey. With the retreat in progress, the worst happened.

On November 16th, Fort Washington in New York fell to the British. Days later on November 20th, Fort Lee was under attack by British and Hessian troops. The Americans abandoned the fort in such haste that they took nothing with them. No food or provisions. No shovels or tools for digging trenches. No extra clothing. No muskets or cannons. Everything was left for the British and the Americans were running for their lives. The British were delighted and believed they could now swiftly end this conflict.

General Howe ordered General Cornwallis to pursue Washington and his army across New Jersey. Cornwallis with an army of 10,000 set out after Washington and the roughly 2,000 men who remained in the Continental Army. Cornwallis said that he would bag Washington, as a hunter bags a fox. In the miserable cold of a pouring rain, Washington was indeed like a fox on the run, and the moment was exactly as Thomas Paine wrote, "These are the times that try men's souls."

If Washington and the army were to survive, reinforcements were needed. Joseph Reed, a Philadelphia lawyer before the war, was Washington's trusted aide. Throughout the long and demoralizing campaign and retreats in New York, Washington had confided in Reed, discussed strategy with him, and expressed his doubts and fears to him. They had ridden together, spent sleepless nights together near the front lines, ate together, and when no food was available hungered together. As a senior member of Washington's staff, Reed took dictation from the general, writing his letters to Congress, telling them of the desperate need from more soldiers, more food, more clothing, more of everything. Washington's orders to his officers were also dictated to Reed, and throughout the retreat, the most urgent orders were sent to General Lee. Washington urged Lee to join him in New Jersey and recombine their forces. Failure to do so could result in annihilation. But unknown to Washington, Reed also had a private correspondence underway with the ambitious General Lee, who believed that he, not Washington, should be commander-in-chief.

As expressed in his private letters to Lee, Reed harshly criticized Washington for being indecisive. Reed believed that Washington dithered too much in making critical decisions. In particular, Reed believed that Washington's hesitancy to abandon New York and indecisions regarding the defense of Fort Washington were responsible in part for the current dire situation. His confidence in Washington was gone, and in its place was fawning praise for General Lee. In one letter to Lee, Reed began by writing, "I do not mean to flatter or praise you at the expense of any other...," then he lavished praise on Lee, while criticizing Washington. Meanwhile, Reed was right in the middle of official correspondence between the two generals.

On November 24th, Washington sent an urgent message to General Lee, saying he must come to New Jersey with all haste. Desperate for help, Washington dispatched Reed to Burlington, New Jersey to urge the governor to send reinforcements. On November 30th, during Reed's absence, a dispatch rider arrived with a letter addressed to Joseph Reed from General Lee. Washington thinking it was Lee's reply to his most recent urgent correspondence opened the letter, and read, "My dear Reed... I received your most obliging, flattering letter... indecision of mind... is a much greater disqualification than stupidity..." Washington's indecision was worse than stupidity; that is what Lee wrote. What Washington thought or felt upon reading these words is unknown. Worse, it was Reed who had obviously initiated this back-stabbing criticism. Reed, his closest confidant, had betrayed his trust, and General Lee, his second in command, had no confidence in his leadership. This clandestine undermining was happening amidst a suffering army threatened daily with a battle that could be its last. How was Washington to respond to such a betrayal by Reed, and treacherous undermining by Lee?

Washington resealed the letter and sent it to Reed with a note of apology. Washington wrote, "The enclosed was put into my hands [by a courier]... Having no idea of it being a private letter... I opened it..." Washington went on to explain his mistake saying, "neither inclination or intention would have prompted me to [open it]." What Reed thought, when he received the opened letter and Washington's note of explanation, is unknown, but for his part, Washington never mentioned the incident. Of course, there is always gossip and other officers learned of Reed's betrayal and urged Washington to take some action, but he refused. Eventually, it all faded and Reed continued in his position on Washington's staff and served him loyally. In fact, Reed named one of his sons, George Washington, because the general, as a man of honor had treated him with honor even though he deserved none.

Honor is like a perfume that is composed of several fragrances that when combined produce a scent that is lovely, sublime, and unique to the person who wears it. For this reason, honor is hard to define, but the underlaying fragrances of honor are well known and easily identified. They are the virtues. Regarding the virtues that make up honor, there is certainly love that sets aside one's personal feelings or comfort in favor of elevating another. Love of this kind requires courage and a strength of character in knowing who you are. Knowing who you are requires a fidelity to truth about God, sin, ourselves, others, and forgiveness. Such truth engenders humility. Love, courage, truth, and humility, each contribute to the perfume of honor. Just as we know a distinctive perfume when we catch its fragrance, we know honor when we see it.

The elders in heaven see God's honor – and his glory and power – and praise him as worthy to receive honor from whom?

From us, who are created in his image, and from all of creation over which he reigns. David tells us that God crowned us with glory and honor. Our Creator bestowed upon us a bit of his honor so that we might see his honor that is present in all of creation and written of in scripture. In return, we are to live an honorable life, practicing all the virtues that combines into a unique signature fragrance that is our honor. While our honor is a mere shadow of God's honor in heaven, we are nevertheless to nurture honor in our character and demonstrate it to others starting with our parents, as stated in the fifth commandment. This commandment carries the promise of a benefit: *so that you may live long in the land the Lord your God is giving you.*" If you break this commandment, does that mean your time in the land will be shortened? Leviticus chapters 18 to 20 answers this question.

These three chapters give the moral code under which the Israelites were to live in the Promised Land. Much of the code addresses sexual morality, but in fact it encompasses all the laws that God gave to the people while in the Sinai Desert. If they failed to obey God's laws, engaged in immorality, and honored vileness, here's what would happen:

"'Keep all my decrees and laws and follow them, so that the land where I am bringing you to live may not vomit you out." (Leviticus 20:22) The message is clear. Reject God's laws, practice immorality, dishonor yourselves, dishonor others, and honor vileness, then the land will vomit you out. If you follow God's commands and honor what God honors, then you are practicing all the virtues – justice, courage, mercy, humility, faith, hope, and love. All these make a society livable, sustainable, peaceful, creative, and prosperous. Sadly, the converse is also true. Honor vileness then all the vices come into the land – injustice, corruption, anger, jealously, immorality, and perversion. A nation that honors vileness cannot endure, and

General Washington's response to Reed's betrayal illustrates why.

Washington did the honorable thing. Even though it was a mistake, he should have never opened a letter addressed to Reed. Therefore, he corrected his mistake and got on with the job of caring for his soldiers and fighting the war. Reed, once exposed, did the honorable thing. He loyally served Washington, which was important, because Reed was good at his job and in that dark hour, Washington needed good men. Roughly, one month after this incident, Washington achieved a great victory at Trenton, when he crossed the icy Delaware River on Christmas night, and attacked the Hessians on the morning of December 26th. This victory gave an enormous boost to the American cause. But, could it have happened, if Washington had gone after Reed for his betrayal?

What if Washington had diverted his attention and effort to humiliating Reed by initiating court martial proceedings, and removing General Lee from command? Some officers would side with Washington, and others with Lee and Reed. The officer corps of the Continental Army would have been divided and further demoralized. It's doubtful they could have pulled off such a daring attack like Trenton. Worse, while the Continental Army fought among themselves, Cornwallis might have captured his fox, Washington, and destroyed the army. The American Revolution would have been over and in a sense, the land would have vomited out the new nation. The importance of honor and honoring the things that God honors are of incalculable importance. What about Americans today? What do we honor? God or vileness?

Diogenes of Sinope (ca. 404 – 323 BC) was a Greek philosopher, who held a lantern up to the faces of his fellow citizens of Athens. He said he wanted to clearly see their faces, because he was searching for an honest man. If Diogenes roamed the halls of the U.S. Capitol, the offices in the White House, the board rooms of major corporations, the faculty clubs at prestigious universities, the hallways of the Department of Justice and the FBI, and movie studios in Hollywood, would he find honorable men and women? If Diogenes brought his lantern into the classrooms of America's seminaries, would he find men and women honoring the things of God? In these multitude of places, would Diogenes find the likes of General Washington or would he find petty, backstabbing Americans, who honor vileness? If honor is so lacking in a nation, will the land not vomit us out? These are sobering and frightening questions. To avoid being vomited out, we must remember two things. First, how God made us and second, our inheritance as Americans.

First remember that honor is intrinsic to God and he crowned us with a bit of it. That's how He made us. We're made for the things of God, who calls us to lead virtuous honorable lives. We're not made to honor vileness. Today more so than at any other time in our nation's history, we can clearly see the misery that comes from honoring vileness. Second, remember who we are as Americans. Whether you trace your ancestry to Jamestown or are a first generation American, as an American citizen, you are a descendent of a pantheon of honorable men and women, who have gone before us, and built a great nation under God. Americans would be among the most wretched people in history, if we cast off God's crown of glory and threw off the robe of honor that previous generations bequeathed to us. Therefore, we must remember how God made us, and remember our unique American heritage of honor so that we may live honorable lives ourselves, and shun those who live dishonorably. Most importantly, we must teach our children the things of God and honor. Then, we may yet save our nation so that our children may *live long in the land the Lord* has given us.

Chapter 9.
JUSTICE... the hallmark of a godly nation

You have wearied the Lord with your words.
"How have we wearied him?" you ask.
By saying, "All who do evil are good in the eyes of the Lord,
and he is pleased with them" or "Where is the God of justice?"
(Malachi 2:17)

Malachi was God's last prophet of the Old Testament. He wrote sometime after 433 B.C. The Children of Israel had returned from their captivity in Babylon, and were living again in the land that God had promised to Abraham, Isaac, and Jacob. What was on God's mind in this final book of the Old Testament? It was justice. God's people were doing evil, and not only condoning it, but they lied to themselves, saying that their actions pleased God. As a consequence, their nation, culture, families, and individuals were in decline. They could see the corruption and societal rot all around them, and it was obviously affecting them, because as their destruction became more apparent, they mocked God asking, *"Where is the God of justice?"* What arrogance! It wearied the Lord.

Is God weary of America and our incessant words about justice even as we do evil and call it good? How many decades now has "No justice, no peace!" been shouted in America's streets? Yet, justice never seems to come and neither does peace. Daily, a multitude of institutions, corporations, and bureaucracies churn out lengthy statements, documents, and regulations on racial justice yet the goal of that justice is like a ship at sea that never docks. A fog of words surround environmental justice, social justice, and the newly created LGBTQ+ justice. Words, words, and more words yet justice never seems to come. America today is like the king in Shakespeare's Hamlet, who cried, "My words fly up, my thoughts remain below: Words without thoughts never to heaven go." Americans have bloviated so much and for so long about justice that the word itself is drained of meaning, and like the king in Hamlet, America's talk of justice are words without thought. What is the source of justice? What are the characteristics and hallmarks of a just nation? What are the differences between just and unjust nations? Can a just nation change into an unjust nation? If so, how does that happen?

The answers we seek will not be found in today's America. The idea and concept of justice has been so mistreated that we will find no truth and no answers by looking at America today. Therefore, we must journey abroad to find the answers we seek, and when we arrive at this place, we will hear testimony not from the living. The dead will speak of justice and injustice. We're going to Paris; the 12th arrondissement to be exact. It's a modest residential district that's south and slightly east of central Paris. A lovely park, Le Bois de Vincennes, is adjacent to our destination yet few tourists venture to where we are going. Our destination is La Cimetière de Picpus. It's an odd name for a cemetery that roughly translates as "flea bite." Let's go there now and hear our witnesses' testimonies of justice and injustice.

* * *

La Cimetière de Picpus, Paris present day

Our Uber driver slows, pulls to the curb, and stops. Through the backseat window, we see a large arched entryway and two massive oak doors that are closed. The doors have that Old World look and charm of being handsomely worn. This type of entry is common around Paris, and behind the doors are typically small courtyards and stairs, leading to apartments. "La cimetière?" we ask our driver skeptically,

"Oui, La Cimetière de Picpus."

We shrug and say, "OK," as we step onto the sidewalk. It's not what we were expecting, but then we didn't know what to expect from such an oddly named cemetery. What's also unexpected is the delightful weather on this late autumn afternoon. The sun hovers on the southern horizon, casting long shadows to remind us that winter is on its way. But, it's as if Paris is saying to winter, "Not today!" The sky is a deep blue, the air is pleasantly cool, and an invigorating breeze quickens our pace, as we push open the heavy oak door and step into the cemetery.

How it got its name is a mystery. One theory is that centuries ago the site was kind of a medieval dermatology clinic, where monks treated skin diseases by pricking the skin that left a mark similar to a flea bite. In French, piquer is the verb "to prick," and "puce" means flea. When the sounds were merged to give "picpus" is a lost footnote in medieval lore. While the origin of the unusual name is uncertain, how this place became a cemetery is dreadfully well documented, and that is why we are here.

Just inside the entrance, we pay the two euro fee to the security guard, who reminds us that the cemetery closes today at 4 PM. We glance at our watch. We only have about an hour, but that should be enough time. La Cimetière de Picpus is large. In fact, it's the second largest private cemetery in Paris, but our purpose is not to tour the entire grounds or stroll among the trees in a section that is like a park. We are here to learn of justice and our visit will entail just four stops. The cemetery chapel, an area named Pits Nos. 1 & 2, and a hero's grave are our first three stops, and for our last stop, we will return to the chapel and enter its splendid sanctuary.

Beyond the entrance we step onto to a cobblestone and gravel plaza that is bordered on one side by an imposing four story building and on the other by a quaint one-story whitewashed *maison.* At the far end of the plaza is our first stop, the cemetery chapel. We don't need to move closer. In fact, its story is best told from a distance, because the story is written into the architecture of the building itself. It's blue painted doors are striking and immediately grabs our attention, but soon our eyes drift skyward toward the copper steeple. It's a weathered green and surprisingly has a clock set into it, making it appear to be more like a cupola atop a bank building rather than a chapel steeple.

The clock seems out of place for a chapel and especially for a chapel in a cemetery, where time has ended. However, the clock is no architectural whimsy or decorative detail. It's meant to convey a profound message. Time no longer matters for those whose mortal remains lie in the grave and the chapel no longer matters either for the church cannot help them. In life they either accepted or rejected Christ, and have been judged in God's court of justice according to their faith. Yet for the living – for the visitors to Picpus – the clock, the chapel, and the grave are immensely important. The grave tells us we are mortal, the chapel tells us we are eternal, and the clock tells us that a moment between mortality and eternity will come when we will be judged.

When the Apostle Paul preached the gospel message to the elite and educated Stoic philosophers in Athens, he ended his sermon saying, *"For he* [God] *has set a day when he will judge the world with justice by the man he has appointed. He has given proof of this to everyone by raising him from the dead."* (Acts 17:31) Not surprisingly, 1st Century Stoic philosophers didn't want to hear about a final divine judgment any more than we do today. After Paul told them that the resurrected Christ would judge the world, the Stoics scoffed, sneered, and abruptly ended the meeting. It's so easy for us to go about our daily routines and never think of eternal judgment, but the one place we cannot avoid it is a cemetery chapel with a clock in its steeple. Time measures the number of days that Our Creator has granted us.

The grave awaits our mortal bodies, and judgment by Christ awaits our eternal souls.

It's a somber and sobering thought, but then that's the point. A final judgment by Christ awakens us to the fact that divine justice governs the lives of nations and individuals. All worldly justice – the laws of nations – are set within an eternal context of divine justice, because justice is an attribute of God and is intrinsic to creation itself. A.W. Tozer, a 20th Century pastor and theologian, wrote, "Justice, when used of God, is a name we give to the way God is … and when God acts justly He is not doing so to conform to independent criterion, but simply acting like Himself in a given situation." (Tozer, The Knowledge of the Holy, p. 87) There is no law library in heaven with shelves of handsomely bound and weighty books. Christ, who will judge us, doesn't send angelic law clerks into the library to research legal precedents on how he should rule. Christ, who is the Son of God, and through whom all things were created, is himself justice, along with righteousness, mercy, grace, love, and all the other attributes of God. (see Colossians 1:15-17) A skilled composer, an artist, an architect, or designer expresses him or herself through their creations, and who they are is visible in their creations. If mortals have this capability, then the attributes of Christ are surely present in all of creation. Therefore, at the center of creation is a perfect and divine justice that rightly judges all people and all nations. (see Psalm 9:19 and Matthew 7:2)

Christ's perfect and divine justice is the starting point of all temporal laws that govern men and nations. The Apostle Paul tells us that the laws by which Christ judges are written into the heart of every man and woman. In his letter to the Romans, Paul wrote, *Indeed, when Gentiles, who do not have the law, do by nature things required by the law, they are a law for themselves, even though they do not have the law. They show that the requirements of the law are written on their hearts, their consciences also bearing witness, and their thoughts sometimes accusing them and at other times even defending them. This will take place on the day when God judges people's secrets through Jesus Christ, as my gospel declares.* (Romans 2:14-16)

Paul's use of the word law refers to Hebrew law, and his point is that even through Gentiles were not given the Mosaic Law written on tablets of stone, they still know what is right and wrong, humane and inhumane, just and unjust, because *the requirements of the law are written on their hearts* and *their consciences also bearing witness.* Therefore, Christ will judge and his judgment will be righteous *for since the creation of the world God's invisible qualities—his eternal power and divine nature—have been clearly seen, being understood from what has been made, so that people are without excuse.* (Romans 1:20)

With the knowledge that Christ's attribute of justice is written in our hearts and the understanding that scripture instructs us on how we are to live justly, humanity is given the challenge, i.e., afforded the free will, to apply Christ's perfect justice on earth. However, because we are mortal, given to sin, and make mistakes, we know from the outset that no justice system set up and administered by men will be perfect. Injustices will always happen yet the goal is to avoid and minimize injustice through devotion to God's laws. Whether an individual or nation seeks or rejects God will determine the degree of justice or injustice in the life of a nation and individuals. Our second stop in Picpus is a case study that illustrates this point.

Pits Nos. 1 & 2 are located toward the rear of the cemetery, and to reach them we must walk through the graveyard that is directly behind the chapel. A gate to the side of the chapel is the entrance. We cross the plaza, open the gate, and follow a gravel path that leads us through an eclectic assembly of mausoleums, crosses, tombstones, and graveyard statuary, all of which bears the weathered stain of time. These centuries old cemeteries are like old growth forests. Both develop organically over time. In old forests, splendid trees grow amid decaying moss covered stumps. So, it is with old cemeteries. Nearby a freshly cleaned mausoleum shines in the sunlight, and just off the gravel path a neglected and overgrown family plot looks lonely. In the distance a cared-for statue of an angel seems as if it could take to flight, and there, near the back wall, a grime covered cherub looks like a dirty toddler. Yet it all comes together in a kind of other world beauty.

Up ahead is the gate to Pits Nos. 1 & 2. We press against it. It is locked, but through its bars, we can see the reason we came here. Beyond the gate is a rectangular walled compound, and in the foreground a square section is covered with gravel. In the center of the gravel stands a monument with a plaque beside it. A grassy section is behind the gravel area, and beyond the grass is another identical gravel covered square. The plaque near the gate is close enough to be read. It says, "Pit No. 2 – 304 martyrs decapitated Place du Trône in June 1794 rest here waiting for the Resurrection." The plaque in the distant gravel area undoubtedly reads similarly. It is Pit No. 1, and it is a mass grave for 1,002 people guillotined in the summer of 1794.

A short walk from these two mass graves is the Place de la Nation. Today, it's a lovely public square with a triumphant statue to the French Republic, but in 1794, this square was known as La Place du Trône, because in 1660 a throne was briefly erected for King Louis XIV on the occasion of his wedding. However, in 1794 from June 13 to July 28, this square became known as La Place du Trône Renversè (The Square of the Reverse Throne). The savage brutality of those six weeks is beyond comprehension. A guillotine was erected in the square, and 1,306 people were beheaded – 197 women and 1,109 men. As many as 55 people were executed in one day. Some were priests, others were Carmelite nuns, and many were nobility, but most – 702 – were identified as "common people." Where do you put this many heads and headless bodies?

The convent of the Canonesses of Saint Augustine was the logical choice. It was close by and had ample space. The ironically named Committee of Public Safety that was controlled by Robespierre seized the convent, and Pit No. 1 was dug. When no more bodies and heads could be squeezed into it, Pit No. 2 was dug. The executions in Place du Trône were only part of the slaughter that was taking place across France in the Reign of Terror. During this roughly eleven month period, between September 1793 to July 1794, an estimated 17,000 were executed and another 10,000 died in prison awaiting trial. This orgy of killing continued until Parisians had enough of Robespierre and he too was sent to the guillotine on July 27, 1794.

The magnitude of violence and scale of injustice during the Reign of Terror is barely comprehensible. How could it have happened? France is today, and certainly was in the 18th Century, a civilized Christian nation, a nation that is the jewel of Western civilization, and known for its art, fashion, cuisine, culture, and enlightenment. How could France of all nations commit such atrocities? A second deeper and more fundamental question is why? Why did France abandon justice and descend into barbarism? The "how" is answered in our next stop, the hero's grave, but the "why" will have to wait to our final stop in the sanctuary. Let's go to the hero's grave. It's easy to find, because the flag of the United States flies above it.

We follow the path back toward the graves and immediately, we see the flag, waving proudly in the breeze. We make our way there. It is a family plot enclosed by a low rail that allows visitors to clearly see the grave, while remaining at a respectful distance. A large tombstone lies flat, covering the entire grave and on it is written, "M. J. P. Y. R. G. D. Lafayette." These initials stand for "Marie – Joseph – Paul – Yves – Roch – Gilbert du Motier, the

Marquis de Lafayette, who was known in America as General Lafayette.

"Lafayette, we are here!" a booming voice shouts, startling us.

We turn to see the security guard, walking on the path. He smiles and gives us a slight wave. We smile, nod, and return our attention to General Lafayette's grave.

The guard's shout is in reference to the flag. On July 4, 1917, Colonel Charles E. Stanton of the U.S. Army visited Lafayette's grave. Three months earlier, America had entered World War I to help war-weary France secure victory. The colonel saw America's part in the war as repayment for France's role in securing America's liberty in the Revolutionary War. Therefore, the colonel at the gravesite said, "Lafayette, we are here," and placed a flag on the general's grave. Since the end of World War I, on each 4th of July a ceremony, attended by both French and American dignitaries, takes place where the old flag is retired and a new one is flown in its place. However, the flag and annual ceremony are not why we are here. We are here to learn Lafayette life's story, and through it gain insight into justice.

When he was eleven years old, Lafayette became the sole heir to one of the largest fortunes in France, and as a teenager, he was a guest at the king's court in Versailles. Despite the privilege of being idly rich, at age nineteen, he commissioned a ship, sailed to America, and became a soldier in the American Revolution. He fought with honor and distinction at the Battle of Brandywine, near Philadelphia, where he suffered a leg wound. He was promoted to major general, received his own command, and led his soldiers in skirmishes with the British throughout Virginia. He attempted to flush out Benedict Arnold's redcoats and engage him in battle, but the traitorous Arnold eluded him. Lafayette's Continental troops played a key role in trapping British General Cornwallis's army in Yorktown, where America won the war. As a high ranking and distinguished officer, Lafayette was acquainted with America's Founding Fathers, and he embraced the American ideals of liberty and justice. Insight into Lafayette's character is afforded by the way George Washington regarded him. Washington, who was much older, treated Lafayette as a father would a son, and the two men shared a lifelong bond of affection and loyalty. At the end of the American Revolutionary War, Lafayette returned to France, and in a few short years, he was again swept up in revolution.

The ideals of liberty advanced in America's revolt against Great Britain's King George III spurred the French toward rebellion of their own, and Lafayette, who was both French aristocracy and a champion of American liberty, was a man for a time such as this. He was a hero in both America and in France. Lafayette was a representative to the Estates-General, and later the National Assembly, and in that parliament, with the assistance of Thomas Jefferson, he was the primary author of France's "The Declaration of the Rights of Man and of the Citizen" that was written in 1789. In the American Revolution, the Declaration of Independence was the seminal document that stated the justification for breaking with Great Britain and forming a new government. Likewise for the French, "The Declaration of the Rights of Man and of the Citizen" served the same purpose.

The American Declaration preamble reads:

"We hold these truths to be self-evident, that all men are created equal, that they are endowed by their Creator with certain unalienable Rights, that among these are Life, Liberty and the pursuit of Happiness. That to secure these rights, Governments are instituted among Men, deriving their just powers from the consent of the governed."

The French Declaration preamble likewise asserts the same justification, which is the natural rights of man. It reads:

"The representatives of the people of France... have resolved to set forth in a solemn declaration, these natural, imprescriptible, and inalienable rights..." The French Declaration similarly follows the American Declaration, stating "that the acts of the legislative and executive powers of government" must respect these natural rights. The American Declaration cites the "Creator" as the author of natural rights, and the French asks for the "blessing and favor" of the "Supreme Being."

The justification for both revolutions was to establish governments that will secure the God-given natural rights of its citizens. The concept of natural rights has a very long history in Western philosophy, tracing its origin to Aristotle. However, no lengthy description of natural rights is needed here, because we've already discussed the concept at our first stop, the chapel. The Apostle Paul stated the Christian understanding of natural rights in his Letter to the Romans. God's law is written in our heart, our conscience bears witness to God's law, and all of creation manifests God law. This the natural law, and the starting point for both the American and French Revolutions were to form governments to secure humanity's God-given natural rights. America, after a failed start with the Articles of Confederation, produced the United States Constitution. France descended into the Reign of Terror that was followed by the Emperor Napoleon, and his wars of conquest. How did such vastly different outcomes happen? Actions taken by France's revolutionary National Assembly tells the tale.

The timeline below documents the Assembly's effort to de-Christianize France.

1789

- August 4: The National Assembly abolishes government support (tithes) of the Roman Catholic Church as part of the "August Decrees." In 18th Century France, as in all European nations, the separation of church and state was a novel concept. With the abolition of tithes, i.e., taxing citizens to pay for the church, France was separating church and state as an act of conscience and justice. If only the revolutionary government had stopped here!

- November 6: The Assembly votes to seize church property and use it to boost France's anemic economy, indicating that the church is seen as a mere institution rather than an ecclesiastical assembly ordained by Christ.

1790

- February 13: The Assembly bans the taking of religious vows, and abolishes contemplative Catholic orders.
- February 23: Parish priests are required to read aloud to their congregations the Assembly's decrees.
- March 12: The sale of church property is approved.
- July 12: The Civil Constitution of the Clergy goes into effect, requiring priests and others to swear an oath of allegiance to the government first and then to God. France's revolutionary government usurped God's authority.

1791

- June 15: Priests are forbidden to wear their robes outside of churches.

1792

- April 5: The Sorbonne is closed due to its fidelity to Catholic doctrine.
- May 27: Priests who have not sworn an oath to the government are ordered deported.
- June 28: Lafayette addresses the Assembly, denouncing their radical policies.
- August 10: The royal palace in Paris is stormed and the monarchy is overthrown.
- September 2: As many as 2,000 prisoners – many who are priests – held in Parisian jails are massacred.

- September 10: Church religious objects made of gold or silver are confiscated.

1793

- January 21: King Louis XVI is executed by guillotine.
- September 17: The Reign of Terror begins.
- October 5: A new calendar is adopted, removing all religious holidays and any reference to saints.
- October 28: All religious instruction by clergy is prohibited.
- November 10: Notre Dame Cathedral is renamed the Temple of Reason, as part of the atheistic Cult of Reason.

1794

- June 8: The festival of the Supreme Being, which was the brain-child of Robespierre, is held with the aim of replacing Christianity.
- June 13- July 28: 1,306 people are guillotined in La Place du Trône Renversè and buried in Pits No. 1 & 2.
- July 28: Robespierre is guillotined and the Reign of Terror ends.

The French Revolution horrifically demonstrates that rejection of God, erasure of Christ from a nation's memory and conscience, and then forcing a secular religion upon the nation brings about the most brutal and inhumane injustices imaginable. French revolutionaries believed they were the enlightened ones, that they were the ones endowed with intellect and reason, and that they would create a new and just society. Instead, because they cut themselves and the nation off from God, who is the source of all justice, the so-called enlightened ones turned France into a hell of injustice, and an orgy of death and destruction. The radical National Assembly's actions document how this happened, but why? Why did civilized, enlightened, cultured, and Christian France descend into such a hell? This is a question of motive and motive involves the spirit of a person and even a nation. Therefore, this question of the spirit is best answered in our next and final stop, the chapel's sanctuary.

We exit the graveyard and step onto the plaza in front of the chapel. This is La Chapelle La Notre Dame de la Paix – The Chapel of Our Lady of Peace – and peace is what we need just now. Picpus is disturbing, and we hope by gaining insight into the why of the Reign of Terror, we will find, certainly not comfort, but perhaps understanding. We open the blue painted chapel door and step inside. The sanctuary is well-lit and welcoming, and we are immediately taken with its reverent simplicity. There is no ornate altar, and very little gilded statuary. Unadorned white walls rise to a vaulted ceiling and in the choir is statue of Christ. To the left is a carved statue of La Notre Dame de la Paix, where Mary is depicted holding a staff in her right hand, and carrying the Christ child in her left arm. Behind the statue is the reason we came inside the chapel. The names, ages, and occupations of all 1,306, who were beheaded and buried in Pits No.1 & 2 are inscribed on the wall. We move closer to get a better look.

Line by line, we scan the list of victims. We pause to read and translate a few entries.

Louise Sibut, married name Liénard, age 50, a domestic
Agathe Greaude, age 19, a seamstress
Louise Fleury, married name Tardy, age 40, a farmer
Martin Alleaume, age 17, a soldier

We reach out, place our hand on the wall, and trace an inscription with our fingers. It's like braille for our hearts. We feel these martyrs. No longer are they anonymous victims of injustice, but are persons with occupations, dreams, hopes, and someone they loved. They were fathers and mothers, brothers and sisters, husbands and wives. Our question of why did France murder these innocent people becomes even more pressing. So we ask, what was the spirit of France during the Reign of Terror?

In his Letter to the Ephesians, the Apostle Paul wrote, *For our struggle is not against flesh and blood, but against the rulers, against the authorities, against the powers of this dark world and against the spiritual forces of evil in the heavenly realms.* (Ephesians 6:12) Only a spirit of evil explains the Reign of Terror, an evil that poisons the hearts and minds of rulers, authorities, and the powerful with intoxicating lies from hell, and those drunk on these lies convince themselves that murdering a maid, a seamstress, a farmer, a soldier, and thirty thousand more souls is, not only just, but good and of benefit to the nation. Now, we must ask how can such a spirit of evil consume rulers, authorities, and the powerful, who were reared and educated in a Christian society and who were almost certainly instructed in the Catholic faith? How can those taught the truth of God be so intoxicated, deluded, and consumed by the lies of evil? Had their mothers or priests never mentioned something as simple as the Golden Rule?

There is only one answer; they – the rulers, the authorities, the powerful – rejected Christ and the church. *They did not think it worthwhile to retain the knowledge of God, so God gave them over to a depraved mind, so that they do what ought not to be done.* (Romans 1:28) They accepted lies as truth, and first lie was there is no God. The radical French revolutionaries were avowed atheists. The second lie was there is no final judgment by Christ. If there is no final divine judgment in heaven's throne room, then there certainly is no earthly justice at the hands of godless men. With God, Christ, truth, and divine judgment rejected, only lies that poison the heart and deprave the mind remain. This is the "why" of the Reign of Terror.

The injustice of the Reign of Terror led to the injustice of Napoleon, which raises a final question: once a nation rejects

God and calls depravity justice, can that nation return to God and become just again? God answered this question through his prophets. Malachi told the ancient Israelites that their evil wearied God. The future looked very bleak for the nation, but then God spoke an amazing message through Malachi. *"I will send my messenger, who will prepare the way before me. Then suddenly the Lord you are seeking will come to his temple; the messenger of the covenant, whom you desire, will come," says the Lord Almighty.* (Malachi 3:1)

Although they had rejected Him, had done evil and unjust things, and society was depraved, God said that the messenger of the covenant, i.e., the promise, who was John the Baptist will come, and he *will prepare the way* for Christ, who *will come to his temple.* The prophet, Ezekiel, foretold that when Christ has come law and justice would return. God said, *I will give them an undivided heart and put a new spirit in them; I will remove from them their heart of stone and give them a heart of flesh.* [20] *Then they will follow my decrees and be careful to keep my laws. They will be my people, and I will be their God.* (Ezekiel 11:19-20) Yes, a nation can return to God. A depraved heart of stone can be changed to flesh. An evil duplicitous mind can receive a new spirit, and justice can be reestablished in a nation.

We glance at our watch. We have spent more time in the sanctuary than we intended and it's almost four o'clock. Picpus will soon close. We take one last look at the 1,306 names on the chapel wall, but our thoughts drift back to Lafayette's grave, and Colonel Stanton's words, "Lafayette, we are here!" With America's entry into World War I, France's enemies quickly crumbled and a great victory over evil was won. When America says, "God, we are here!" then the forces of evil that war against America will crumble and a great victory over injustice will be won. As we turn to leave, we whisper a prayer, "Lord may every American, everyday declare with conviction, 'God, we are here!'" The day that America prays this prayer is the day that justice will become an American virtue again.

Chapter 10.
CIVILITY... in the smallest of books
and the greatest of men

³ When we put bits into the mouths of horses to make them obey us, we can turn the whole animal. ⁴ Or take ships as an example. Although they are so large and are driven by strong winds, they are steered by a very small rudder wherever the pilot wants to go. ⁵ Likewise, the tongue is a small part of the body, but it makes great boasts. Consider what a great forest is set on fire by a small spark. ⁶ The tongue also is a fire, a world of evil among the parts of the body. It corrupts the whole body, sets the whole course of one's life on fire, and is itself set on fire by hell. (James 3:3-6)

The biggest things in life depend upon the smallest things. That's what James, who was Jesus' half-brother and an important leader in the early church, is telling us in his New Testament letter. In the above passage, he contrasts the smallness of the tongue with the outsized damage it can cause. In his letter, he also offers insight into other small things that result in big things. Listening is a small thing that we can all do, and we know that not listening can have major consequences. James advises that: *Everyone should be quick to listen, slow to speak, and slow to become angry.* (1:19) He also instructs us on doing: *Show me your faith without deeds, and I will show you my faith by what I do.* (2:18) The doing involves small things such as: being respectful, behaving modestly, and showing mercy. He also tells us what wisdom looks like. Wisdom *is first of all pure; then peace-loving, considerate, submissive, full of mercy and good fruit, impartial and sincere.* (3:17) Toward the end of his short letter, he talks of humility: *Humble yourselves before the Lord, and he will lift you up.* (4:10) Humility also extends to judging others: *But you – who are you to judge your neighbor?* (4:12)

Are not all these small things? Things of behavior and character that we are all capable of doing and yet so often we don't. We all know that not doing these small things can cause problems or embarrassment. No one likes to hear, "You aren't even listening to me!" And, this declaration is invariably followed by a complaint and perhaps an argument. From experience, we all know that small things affect situations in our lives, but are small things that we do or don't do responsible for charting the entire course of our lives? James tells us that the tongue, as small as it is, *sets the whole course of one's life on fire.* What about other small things? Being respectful, behaving modestly, showing mercy, being sincere, acting with humility – can these small things set the course of our lives, sending us in one direction if we do them and in another if we don't? What about a nation? Now, that's really big! Can these small things set the course for an entire nation? The answer to these questions are found in the most unlikely of places. The answers are in the gift shop at the home of America's Founding Father, George Washington. Let's go now to Mount Vernon.

* * *

Mount Vernon in Virginia, present day

Mount Vernon is always busy. The parking lots are filled with cars from seemingly every state in the Union. Lines of buses wait to pick up the hundreds of students, who are on their school's Washington, D.C. tour. Not surprisingly, the gift shop is crowded. We make our way past the display cases packed with George Washington keychains, Martha Washington greeting cards, and bobble-head dolls of both George and Martha. Without stopping, we pass racks stocked with Mount Vernon coffee mugs, water bottles, dishtowels, placemats, and so much more! The books at the back of the store are our destination, and the shelves brim with a weighty mixture of thick biographies, detailed histories of the American Revolution, and numerous large coffee table books with stunning pictures of Mount Vernon in each of the four seasons. None of these are what we're looking for. We're searching for a book about small things, and there it is; we've spotted it. Not surprisingly, it's the smallest book on the shelf and easily overlooked.

Small is an overly generous descriptor for this book. Tiny is more accurate yet the title is long. It is: "George Washington's Rules of Civility & Decent Behaviour in Company and Conversation." The books consists of 110 rules to instruct a gentleman or gentlewoman on how to behave. Some are quaint and humorous by today's standards:

9ᵗʰ Spit not in the fire, nor stoop low before it. Neither put your hands into the flames to warm them, nor set your feet upon the fire, especially if there be meat before it.

13ᵗʰ Kill no vermin, or fleas, lice, ticks etc. in the sight of others...

100ᵗʰ Cleanse not your teeth with the table cloth napkin, fork, or knife; but if others do it, let it be done with a pick tooth.

101ˢᵗ Rinse not your mouth in the presence of others.

In this age of COVID, another of Washington's 110 rules is spot-on.

5ᵗʰ If you cough, sneeze, sigh, or yawn, do it not loud but privately; and speak not in your yawning, but put your handkerchief or hand before your face and turn aside.

Washington was also aware that we should not bore others.

80ᵗʰ Be not tedious in discourse or in reading unless you find the company pleased therewith.

The 1ˢᵗ rule, however, reveals Washington's character and provides context for interpreting all subsequent 109 rules, even the ones that today we find odd or funny. Washington's first rule of behavior is this:

1ˢᵗ Every action done in company ought to be with some sign of respect to those that are present.

Here is evidence of Washington's humility. In fact, most of the rules are associated with humble self-respect and respect for others. Further, Washington's rules come from the same biblical wisdom that James relied upon in writing his letter. Consider the following rules:

44ᵗʰ When a man does all he can though it succeeds not well blame not him that he did it.

48ᵗʰ Wherein you reprove another be unblameable yourself, for example is more prevalent than precepts.

Washington's final rule is this:

110ᵗʰ Labour to keep alive in your breast that little celestial fire called conscience.

The most remarkable aspect of the rules is that Washington wrote them when he was 14 years-old.

The foreword to the book tells us that young Washington developed these rules "from an English translation of a French book of maxims and were intended to polish manners, keep alive the best affections of the heart, impress the obligation of moral virtues, teach how to treat others in social relations, and above all, inculcate the practice of a perfect self-control." Biographers are uncertain as to why Washington as a boy wrote these rules. Some believe it was simply an exercise in penmanship, but what is undeniable is that Washington throughout his life was the epitome of good manners and self-control. To go one step farther and conclude that these 110 rules show that at an early age and throughout his life Washington was a humble man requires clarification, and with this clarification comes the answers to our questions: Are small things that we do or don't do responsible for charting the entire course of our lives? What about the course of a nation? Washington's life provides the answers.

Washington's rules of civility and decent behavior show that even at 14 years of age, he was well aware of the feelings of others, that he wanted others to have a favorable opinion of him, and that he was aware of social standing. In the 18th Century, your name, your family, a good reputation, and appropriate manners, along with your wealth and property, all contributed to your social standing, and there was a definite societal hierarchy. There is little need to point out that today we live in an upside-down world, where good manners and integrity count for little, and are sometimes viewed as handicaps to success. In modern America, manners exist to be broken. The vilest, coarsest, and crudest behavior is celebrated today, but that was not the case in Washington's era.

Even as a boy and certainly as a young man, he was aware of the Washington family's social standing. He was also very ambitious, but there was a problem. Among the Colonial Virginia planter class, the Washington's were not at or near the top. Their wealth and land did not compare to that of the Carter, Custis, or Fairfax families. When George was eleven, his father died, and he was raised by his mother in a six-room farmhouse near Fredericksburg, Virginia. One of seven children, George's family certainly was not poor. They owned 10,000 acres scattered among various farms, but the widow Washington was also not high in social status compared to the Tidewater planters. For example, George did not have the opportunity to attend the College of William and Mary, as many sons in the planter class did.

He received only the equivalent of a grade school education, and despite all his accomplishments, this bothered him all his life. Further, George, being one of the younger children, had no prospects of inheriting land, but when his older brother,

Lawrence, died of tuberculosis, that changed. With Lawrence's passing, George inherited a 2,500 acre plantation named Mount Vernon. Then in 1759, George married up. The widow Martha Custis brought to the marriage, land, wealth, and a higher social standing, but even before the marriage, Washington's reputation was growing.

In 1754, the Virginia House of Burgesses raised a militia, and Lt. Colonel Washington was selected to the lead them. The French and Indian War was underway, and in 1755 at the Battle of Monongahela, Washington distinguished himself for bravery, calmness in battle, and leadership. He had two horses shot out from under him, and after the battle, it was learned that four musket balls had pierced his great coat yet he was unharmed. This battle seemed to foreshadow the legendary greatness of Washington's military career as Commander in Chief of the Continental Army. From crossing the icy Delaware River for the surprise Christmas attack at Trenton, New Jersey, to the desperate winter at Valley Forge, and onto victory at Yorktown, Washington held the rag-tag army together and defeated the British army, which was the world's premier military power.

Did the small things – the things that the 14 year-old boy wove into 110 rules – set the course of Washington's life, allowing him to achieve all that he did as a husband, a step-father to Martha's children, a planter, an elected Virginia representative, a general, a statesman, and as president? Washington's fellow representatives at the Virginia Convention in 1774 thought so. The purpose of the Convention was to debate the colonies' worsening relationship with Britain, and elect seven delegates to represent Virginia in the Continental Congress. Washington and Patrick Henry were among the seven elected delegates. Henry was known for his eloquence and firebrand speeches, as demonstrated by his famous "give me liberty or give me death" speech. Historian, Joseph J. Ellis in his book entitled,

"His Excellency," wrote that Washington's "fellow burgesses knew that Henry could be counted on to say the magnificent thing, whereas Washington could be counted on to say little, but do the right thing." The trust that Washington's contemporaries placed in him was a mark of his character.

Only a man of remarkable character and integrity could have held the Continental Army together during the hardships suffered at Valley Forge and throughout the long years of the Revolutionary War. Washington was a strict disciplinarian. He did not hesitate to hang deserters and order lashes for soldiers not following orders or breaking rules. Fear of punishment was a fact of life in Washington's army, but fear alone does not win the day and motivate men to go above and beyond the call of duty. Respect and admiration for the officer giving the orders are required, and these are earned every day through small things. How the officer carries himself, the words he chooses to use, the respect he shows to those in the lowest ranks, demonstrating kindness, and showing mercy. In other words, all the things in Washington's 110 rules and more! What emerges is a man, who exhibits the highest virtue which is humility.

To say that Washington was a humble man seems contrary to historical evidence. In fact, Washington – according to his contemporary political detractors – was obsessed with his social standing. He paid careful attention to his appearance, his reputation, and to what others were saying about him. This does not sound like a humble man until you dig deeper and have a fuller understanding of humility. The place to look for that understanding is the Bible.

The Bible tells us that: *Now Moses was a very humble man, more humble than anyone else on the face of the earth.* Numbers 12:3) God chose Moses and he was a man of destiny, charged with the responsibility of leading his people to freedom. Likewise, Washington was a man of destiny, given the seemingly impossible task of leading his people to freedom. This Moses – Washington comparison is not intended to equate their relationship to God; Moses was called "a friend of God." That never applied to Washington. However, there is commonality in their leadership. They were moral, incorruptible, stern when discipline was required, and merciful when men needed mercy. Even as a child, we see mercy in Washington's 44th rule: *When a man does all he can though it succeeds not well blame not him that he did it.* A merciful man is one who looks upon another person with undeserved compassion and grants pardon. The virtue of mercy springs only from a humble heart that feels another's suffering and identifies with their predicament. Is this not a small thing that is monumentally big?

Through Washington's life, we see that small things are big things, and small things do set the course of one's life. It's not a stretch to conclude that the small things woven into Washington's character were instrumental in securing a big thing – the freedom of our nation. But, why are small things so important? Why do manners, modesty in speech, dress, and behavior, and respect for others have such seemingly outsized importance? Because they are rooted in God's law and when obediently followed, God blesses the person and the nation that follows his law.

The Bible, of course, says nothing about which fork to use at dinner, or that a gentleman rises when a lady enters the room, but these and other Western social conventions accepted as societal norms can be traced back to respect for others and importantly, respect for yourself. Moreover, respect is based on deeper truths such as honesty, e.g., *thou shalt not bear false witness against thy neighbor*, and avoiding jealously, e.g., *thou shalt not covet thy neighbor's house.* (Exodus 20:16-17) These are only two of the Ten Commandments. With the other eight, they are the foundation of our attitude and behavior toward God and others.

Then, in the Sermon on the Mount, and in particular the Beatitudes, Jesus teaches us a higher moral standard of behavior and attitude toward God and others. *Blessed are the merciful, for they shall obtain mercy. Blessed are the pure in heart; for they shall see God.* (Matthew 5:7-8) Just as delicious grapes mark the character of a wine and vineyard, the fruits of humble civility marks the character of a person and a people.

Could Washington have practiced his last rule without first living into Rule #1? The two rules are:

1st Every action done in company ought to be with some sign of respect to those that are present.

110th Labour to keep alive in your breast that little celestial fire called conscience.

These rules work in unison. The "celestial fire of conscience" only burns in a person with self-respect and who is respectful to others. Small things do set the course of one's life, and the sum total of small things that a society deems acceptable and unacceptable sets the course of a nation.

Today, American society is vile and vulgar. We're as far from Washington's rules of civility and behavior as heaven is from hell, and there is no need to provide examples to document this conclusion. We live every day in a sewer of incivility. Therefore, rather than looking backwards, and asking how did we get to such an appalling state, let's look forward, and ask: can we keep the big things of life, such our freedom, rights, and liberty, while failing to practice the little things of life, such as civility? We've kept our freedom for almost 250 years, but then no previous American generation has been so morally and spiritually bankrupt, as demonstrated by our current lack of respect for ourselves and others.

A free people must practice self-disciple in order to remain free, and self-disciple requires a philosophical, ethical, moral, and spiritual code that guides the nation. The vast majority of citizens must consent to live under and be governed by the code. It doesn't mean that everyone has to agree with the code or believe in its precepts, but it does mean that everyone acknowledges that the code exists and that it defines what is good and what is evil, what is lawful and what is unlawful, what is acceptable and unacceptable behavior, which includes manners, modesty, reputation, and all the things we have discussed. For America, and indeed all of Western civilization, our code is Judeo-Christianity. Now, we are at the heart of the issue. Obedience to biblical truth brings God's blessings both for the individual and for the nation. Freedom is God's blessing, and obedience to God's truth sustains freedom.

Can the generations of Americans alive today sustain our freedom? Can we live into the promise and dream that is America and entrust that the promise and dream live for future generations? Yes! Absolutely yes! Where shall we begin this great and important work? With the small things – good manners, modesty in speech and dress, a reputation for honesty and integrity, and most importantly, respect for ourselves and others. Everyone regardless of education, income, race, religion, ethnic group, etc. can resolve to do these things, and to teach their children the value of them. James' in his letter told us: .... *take ships as an example. Although they are so large and are driven by strong winds, they are steered by a very small rudder wherever the pilot wants to go.* The largest things in life are indeed dependent upon the smallest things – our own self-control and civility.

Chapter 11.
GRATITUDE... *makes the heart well*

[11] Now on his way to Jerusalem, Jesus traveled along the border between Samaria and Galilee. [12] As he was going into a village, ten men who had leprosy met him. They stood at a distance [13] and called out in a loud voice, "Jesus, Master, have pity on us!"

[14] When he saw them, he said, "Go, show yourselves to the priests." And as they went, they were cleansed.

[15] One of them, when he saw he was healed, came back, praising God in a loud voice. [16] He threw himself at Jesus' feet and thanked him—and he was a Samaritan.

[17] Jesus asked, "Were not all ten cleansed? Where are the other nine? [18] Has no one returned to give praise to God except this foreigner?" [19] Then he said to him, "Rise and go; your faith has made you well." (Luke 17:11-19)

What is Jesus talking about – *your faith has made you well*? By the time the grateful Samaritan returned to Jesus, his leprosy was already cured, and likewise the other ungrateful nine were also cured. For all ten, the disease that afflicted their flesh was gone. They were lepers no more, but only this one man was made well and his wellness was a result of the change in his heart, not the change in his flesh. What made his heart well was faith expressed as praise and thanksgiving to God. This Samaritan had a grateful heart. Gone was the rot of self-absorption, worldly priorities, and ingratitude that gripped the hearts of the other nine, preventing them from returning to Jesus and praising God. Jesus cured the flesh of all ten, and the faith of the one Samaritan made his heart well. His heart had a new wellness of gratitude. The other ungrateful nine missed the opportunity to be both cured and made well.

Today, modern medicine has the power to cure many diseases, including leprosy, but what it cannot do is make the human heart well. There is no pharmaceutical that can soften a hard heart. There is no surgical procedure that cuts selfishness out of the human character, and there is no radiation therapy that shrinks a bloated ego. A good doctor, a truthful doctor tells his patients that it is not he who heals. His role as physician is to provide treatment that allows the body to heal itself. So it is with the Great Physician. Jesus, who takes away the sin of the world, provides forgiveness that allows the good things, the virtuous things, the godly things that Our Creator put into the human heart at Creation to become active, vibrant, and robust. With sin forgiven, gratitude like an ointment covers the heart, signaling its healing. From a well heart comes thanksgiving, happiness, and peace, and what is true for an individual is also true for a nation. A nation that offers thanksgiving to God is a happy nation; it is a nation whose heart is well.

In the gospel account, the story of the ten lepers ends with the return of the one. We don't know what the grateful Samaritan did next, but let's imagine that he went to find the other nine and urge them to go and thank Jesus so that they too might share in his wellness. Gracious hearts do that sort of thing. While we have to imagine what happened next in the biblical story, we don't have to imagine what happened in America. A most gracious woman spent decades of her life urging presidents, governors, senators, and government officials to set aside the fourth Thursday in November as a national day of thanksgiving to God.

She was the most extraordinary of women. She defined good taste. Hostesses followed her instructions for the perfect dinner. Homes across America were furnished and decorated according to her style, and she even influenced the architectural design of houses. As if all this were not enough, she was also a poet, who penned the famous nursery rhyme "Mary Had a Little Lamb."

Let's go now and meet this amazing woman, who earnestly believed that if America was to be a truly well nation, it first must be a grateful nation, thanking God for a multitude of blessings. However, we must approach her with quiet circumspection. It's an extremely difficult time for her. The year is 1822, her husband has recently died, and her fifth child is only a few weeks old.

* * *

Newport, New Hampshire, late autumn 1822.

Sarah Josepha Hale adjusted the wick of the oil lamp on the writing desk. The flame brightened and illuminated the papers spread in front of her, but it left untouched the late night shadows that lurked in the corners. The room was small, but the light was feeble, and that's exactly the way Sarah felt. Small, feeble, and surrounded by shadows. Her beloved husband, David, was not long in the grave – a little more than month. Yet that was enough time for Sarah's new reality to sink in. She was a 34 year-old widow with five children. The oldest, David Jr., was only 7, and the youngest, William, was newly born. Then, there was Horatio who was 5, Frances 3, and Sarah 2. Lovingly, Sarah gently ran her fingers along the edge of the desk worn smooth by time and use. This was David's desk – David Hale, Esq. to be precise. The income from his law practice was more than ample for their large family, but that was no more. What was she to do?

This desk, however, was also her desk and at night when David and the children were asleep, she often crept into the office and wrote poetry. Tonight as the nights since he died, there would be no writing. Her muse was in mourning too, and the verses that Sarah had penned weeks earlier now seemed to mock her. This volume of poems was almost finished, and it was entitled, *The Genius of Oblivion*. What an ironic title! Was that her destiny? Oblivion? How was a widow to support herself and five young children? The millinery shop that she opened was failing. The shop was only weeks old, but she knew it wasn't going to make it, and her heart wasn't in running a business. So what next? Her poetry? She could not name a single female writer or poet, who was even published much less earned enough money from scribbling to feed a family. Should she work in her father's tavern, The Rising Sun? Who would look after the children or nurse William? Should she return to teaching school? The pay would not be enough to feed her children. She glanced at the bank promissory note on the desk that some people called checks. David's brothers in the Masonic Lodge had brought it over this morning. They urged her to use some of the money to publish her poetry. They were sure it would be a success. She was not so convinced. She picked up the check, walked to the window, and stared into the darkness.

The New England autumn that year had been gorgeous. The days crisp and bright. Then, David suddenly died and all the colorful beauty vanished too. The trees that only weeks ago were clothed in golden and red hues now stood in the darkness as stark and bare as skeletons. Yet as she continued to gaze out the window, the eastern sky began to brighten, giving the first hint of a new day. The barren trees now standing in silhouette against a strengthening morning light took on a new and different kind of beauty. Perhaps, in her own life a new dawn will come, and the stark barrenness of her mourning will be transformed into a new kind of beauty. For the first time in weeks, she felt encouraged.

She extinguished the lamp, went upstairs to her and David's bedroom, washed her face in the basin, and donned the black dress of mourning that she had worn since the funeral. As the room began to brighten with the morning light, she decided that she would take the advice of David's Freemason brothers and publish her poems. She would get on with life, and as she buttoned her dress, she made another decision. Some women wore black for a year after their husband's passing. She would wear black every day for the rest of her life, and never forget the love she and David shared.

The Genius of Oblivion was published the next year in 1823, and with continued help from family and the Freemasons, Sarah held the family together. She also continued to write. Four years later, her first novel, *Northwood; or, Life North and South* was published in the U.S. and also in England under the title, *A New England Tale*. For the 1800's, it was a remarkable book. First, a woman author in the 19th Century was a rarity, and second, the novel touched on the moral issue of slavery. It would be another 15 years before Harriet Beecher Stowe's *Uncle Tom's Cabin* would be published. The success of *Northwood* caught the attention of Reverend John Blake, the Boston publisher of the *Ladies' Magazine*, and Sarah was soon hired as the magazine's editor. A female editor – even for a woman's magazine – was unusual in 1828, which prompted John Neal, a writer for *The Yankee*, to refer to "he-editors" and "she-editors." Sarah, however, preferred the title "editress."

While editress, Sarah continued to write poetry and in 1830, her collection entitled, *Poems for Our Children* was published. The nursey rhyme "Mary Had a Little Lamb" was part of this collection. This favorite children's poem may have been inspired by an event that took place when Sarah was teaching school in her home town of Newport, New Hampshire. In 1833, shortly after *Poems for Our Children* was published Sarah founded the Seaman's Aid Society in Boston that provided a boarding house for sailors and employment for the wives of sailors as seamstresses. In addition to caring about her fellow Bostonians, Sarah was very patriotic. Her father, Captain Gordon Buell, was an officer in the Revolutionary War, and this no doubt contributed to her lifelong patriotism. She was a strong advocate for the preservation of George Washington's Mount Vernon, and she was instrumental in raising money to complete the Bunker Hill Monument in Boston.

In 1837, Louis Antoine Godey of Philadelphia, the owner and publisher of *Godey's Lady's Book,* bought the *Ladies' Magazine*, merged the two publications, and named Sarah as editress. With 150,000 subscribers, *Godey's Lady's Book* was one of the most influential periodicals in the nation. Sarah was not only the editress, but a prolific contributor. Her writing accounted for half the content in some editions. She wrote on a variety of topics, including family life, proper manners, good taste, and "domestic science" that covered items of interest to 19th Century housewives. While these topics sold magazines, Sarah also wrote about more enduring and consequential subjects. She was a strong advocate for educating women, and much of her writing chronicled the role of women in advancing a moral and Christian society modeled after New England Puritan values. She wrote that women were "God's appointed agent of morality," and she said, "There is no influence so powerful as that of the mother." However, her greatest contribution to the fabric of American life was her unflagging determination to have the fourth Thursday in November set aside as a day of thanksgiving to "offer to God our tribute of joy and gratitude for the blessings of the year."

Sarah's campaign for thanksgiving began in 1836 and it did not end until President Lincoln made his "Thanksgiving Proclamation" in 1863. During those 37 years, Sarah wrote to Presidents Zachary Taylor, Millard Fillmore, Franklin Pierce, James Buchanan, and of course Abraham Lincoln. Undoubtedly, America's pain and suffering during the Civil War motivated Lincoln's proclamation. In July of 1863, the Union Army had won a great victory at Gettysburg, but this victory had come at the staggering cost of more than 50,000 casualties. Gettysburg signaled that the Union would prevail in the war, and to Lincoln it also pointed to the need for the nation to heal.

In his Thanksgiving Proclamation issued on October 3, 1863, Lincoln wrote, "I... fervently implore the interposition of the Almighty Hand to heal the wounds of the nation and to restore it as soon as may be consistent with the Divine purposes to the full enjoyment of peace, harmony, tranquility and Union." Lincoln recognized that these are the fruits of a grateful nation, but it took the prompting of Sarah's letter for the president to take action.

Sarah believed that thanksgiving makes a nation well. Decades before the conflict of the Civil War began, she recognized the divisions between North and South, and she wrote about the dehumanizing and moral consequences of slavery for both the African slaves and the owners, who held them in bondage. She hoped that getting America to focus on God's blessings might be the start of bringing the nation together, healing divisions, and making America well. In an 1835 essay entitled, "Thanksgiving of the Heart," she wrote, "There is a deep moral influence in these periodical seasons of rejoicing in which a whole community participates." Thanks to Sarah Josepha Hale, America from 1863 until today has a periodical season of rejoicing. Gratitude makes the heart of an individual and the heart of a nation well.

One hundred and sixty Thanksgivings have passed since President Lincoln's proclamation. In 1924, Macy's held its first Thanksgiving Day Parade, promising all who watched it "a marathon of mirth." In 1939, President Roosevelt signed a proclamation changing the date from the fourth Thursday in November to the next to last Thursday. Roosevelt's goal was to kick-off the Christmas shopping season early as a boost to the economy during The Great Depression. The date change, however, created confusion, and in 1942, Roosevelt in a new proclamation reverted to the original date of the fourth Thursday.

Today, Macy's parade still rolls through the streets of New York, Thanksgiving continues to mark the beginning of the

Christmas retail season with Black Friday sales, and football remains an important part of the holiday tradition. An equal tradition is the annual lamenting of the commercialization of Thanksgiving and Christmas. Yet all of these things are part of who we are – or were – as Americans, and a day of national thanksgiving is just as Sarah intended – a day to bring the nation together to heal wounds. This healing happens because thanksgiving to God makes the heart well, and well hearts seek "peace, harmony, tranquility and Union," just as President Lincoln said in his proclamation. But, what of America's heart today? How well is it?

Who does America today more resemble, the grateful Samaritan who praised God, or the ungrateful nine who didn't brother to even thank Jesus? The answer is self-evident. America is among the ungrateful nine, and perhaps our ingratitude explains why America is so divided. The accepted explanation for America's rancorous division is attributed to politics, race, class, education, sexual orientation, and the list could go on. But, perhaps the real reason for this troubled time has a simple explanation – unwell hearts due to ingratitude.

In the Lord's Prayer, Jesus taught us gratitude for our daily bread. We are to pray, "Give us this day our daily bread." In this simple statement our dependency upon God and our gratitude to him are beautifully woven together. Gratitude begins with acknowledging our dependency upon God, or stated conversely, renouncing the supremacy of ourselves. This acknowledgement, however, is only the first dose of the treatment that makes our hearts well. All ten lepers certainly acknowledged that they were dependent upon Jesus to heal them. Otherwise, they would not have been shouting, *"Jesus, Master, have pity on us!"* When we are humble, dependent upon God, and have faith, Jesus said, *"Ask and it will be given to you; seek and you will find; knock and the door will be opened to you."* (Luke 11:9) America's troubles and divisions can be healed, but we have to ask humbly with faith. This is the first dose of Jesus' treatment that cures us. The second dose is what makes us well.

Only one of the lepers received the second dose that makes our hearts well. Only one expressed gratitude, praised God, and offered thanksgiving, and only one's heart was made well. Why something as simple as gratitude makes our hearts well is not a mystery. Jesus tells us the answer in the Lord's Prayer. The next line after "Give us this day our daily bread," is "and forgive us our debts, as we forgive our debtors." (Matthew 6:12) A gracious heart is a forgiving heart. A forgiving heart is a well heart that is filled with gratitude. Gratitude and forgiveness are the ointments that heal divisions, offers peace, seeks harmony, and desires tranquility. Gratitude makes the heart well and can heal a nation.

America's economic, physical, spiritual, and moral wounds from the Civil War were deep and grievous, and in the midst of this turmoil, President Lincoln at Sarah's urging, called for thanksgiving to God, and the nation began to heal and to be made well. After the Civil War, Sarah, reflecting on Thanksgiving, wrote, "The idea was very near to my heart, for I believed that this celebration would be a bond of union throughout the country, as well as a source of happiness in the homes of the people." Gratitude makes the heart well, and when Americans are once again grateful, our wounds will begin heal.

Sarah Josepha Hale remained editress of *Godey's Lady's Book* until 1877. She did not retire until the age of ninety. Two years later, she died in her Philadelphia home that today is marked with an historical plaque. During her long and prolific career, she wrote many books, including *A Complete Dictionary of Poetical Quotations* that was published in 1860. The lines below are excerpted from that book, and they are a fitting way to conclude our visit with Sarah, whose heart was indeed well and filled with gratitude.

O, beautiful rainbow; - all woven of light!
There's not in thy tissue, one shadow of night;
Heaven surely is open when thou dost appear,
And, bending above thee, the angels draw near,
And sing, - "The rainbow! the rainbow!
"The smile of God is here."

Surely when Sarah, after her long and gracious life, entered heaven's gate, God smiled and told her that, while she had worn black everyday of her life, it was now time for bright and joyful colors. Her beloved David was waiting for her and her mourning for him was at an end. No doubt, Sarah praised God with thanksgiving.

Chapter 12.
WISDOM... in the house of mourning

The heart of the wise is in the house of mourning... (Ecclesiastes 7:4)

Mourning means loss, sadness, and a wound to the soul that causes emotional, spiritual, and even physical suffering. Yet King Solomon, who was reputed to be the wisest man in the ancient world, tells us that wisdom is found *in the house of mourning*. A funeral wake is held in a house that mourns, and in its rooms are hushed conversations and tearful moments that are mingled with laughter and joy, because life is both bitter and sweet, and mourning is a time for remembering both. The house itself stands as witness to the life that was lived in it; both the good and the bad, the noble and the crass, the kind and the malevolent. Therefore, the scent of memories fill the house of mourning, and one particular fragrance is so gentle and subtle that not everyone takes note of it. It is the scent of the eternal, a whiff of heaven, that opens the eyes of the heart to see what the eyes of the mind cannot or will not see. Together the eyes of the heart with the eyes of the mind sharpen reason, guide thoughts, offer perspective, and form conclusions about life and lives lived that astound others. This is wisdom. It is sensing and responding to the eternal even as the temporal demands all the attention and urges action. The person, whose heart *is in the house of mourning*, senses the fragrance of the eternal among the overpowering confusion of temporal smells. The wise person rises above the confusion to offer wisdom.

Such a high sounding metaphorical description of wisdom begs for a real-life example that illustrates its veracity. Fortunately, we have one. The story of this wise man, whose heart was in the house of mourning begins on the National Mall in Washington, D.C. Let's go there now and hear his story.

* * *

The National Mall, Washington, D.C. present day

In the center of the Mall is the Washington Monument. The slender white obelisk points to the heavens and its capstone is topped with an aluminum tip that is inscribed with the words "Laus Deo" – Praise be to God. It is a fitting tribute to Our Founding Father, and an apt representation of America's aspiration for the future, and thankfulness for our blessings of the past for which God alone is to be praised. Just off the Mall on a quiet tidal basin sits the Jefferson Memorial. Granite steps rise from the water's edge and lead into a circular temple made of white marble. Handsome Ionic columns support the dome, and underneath it, a large bronze statue of Jefferson dominates the center of the memorial. The statue depicts Jefferson standing with his head held high, as if he were summoning all his vast knowledge in debate of a great idea. The walls of Jefferson's temple are inscribed with his words from the Declaration of Independence. Above and encircling the base of the dome is his declaration against tyranny. It reads, "I have sworn upon the altar of God eternal hostility against every form of tyranny over the mind of man."

Surely both Washington and Jefferson were wise men, and their marvelous and impressive monuments are testaments to the lasting wisdom of their lives. However, we seek a monument and memorial that represents a house of mourning, and the Washington and Jefferson Memorials are not that. Therefore, we must look elsewhere and our journey takes us to the western end of the Mall near the Potomac River. There we find the Lincoln Memorial.

Like the memorials to Washington and Jefferson, Lincoln's is majestic, impressive, commanding, and a fitting tribute to America's 16th president. It too is a temple, but not like Jefferson's domed temple that displays the lightness, elegance, and gracefulness of a master architect, who loved knowledge and ideas. That was Jefferson, but not Lincoln. His memorial is massive, solid, weighty, and somber. It is patterned after the Parthenon in Athens, and fitting of a Greek temple; tall steps must be ascended to enter. A visitor might anticipate that the statue of this victorious wartime president is triumphantly standing, savoring his victory and accomplishments. Instead, the visitor finds an overpoweringly large statue of Lincoln that has him seated. His head is slightly downcast, his deeply lined faced is thoughtful, and his downward gaze is unfixed, as if he is pondering a fateful decision. We know the decisions that were thrust upon Lincoln were painful, sorrow ridden, and difficult.

Throughout Lincoln's presidency, America was at war with itself. Like a family contesting the will of a rich relative and fighting viciously over the estate, we were a family torn apart. In this bitterest of family fights, it is the executor, who must settle the estate, bring peace, and ultimately healing to the family that mourns the loss of what once was, while fighting over what will be. Lincoln was the nation's executor. His presidency over a divided nation is his house of mourning, and the wisdom of his heart is memorialized in his temple on the National Mall.

The interior of the memorial is divided into three chambers that are separated by Greek columns. In the central chamber is the seated statue of Lincoln, who is pondering the weighty decisions he must make. In the chambers to either side on the north and south are the examples of Lincoln's wisdom that we seek. They are easy to find. They are chiseled into the white marble walls. The south chamber is inscribed with Lincoln's Gettysburg Address – all 272 words of that speech. Carved into the wall of the north chamber is his Second Inaugural Address, and it too is very brief. It took only about five minutes to deliver. Here is our first insight – wisdom does not require lengthy dialog. Wisdom is truth that speaks to both the heart and the mind, and it requires no drawn-out explanations. To help absorb the wise truth of Lincoln's speeches, highly allegorical murals hang above each address. They are large – 60 feet by 12 feet – and each mural references eternity. Let's go into the south chamber to find Lincoln's wisdom in his Gettysburg Address.

The Civil War stunned the nation. For the first time, photographs of the aftermath of battles were published. This new technology of photography captured the carnage, destruction, suffering, and the loss of human life in ways that artists' sketches could not match. Grainy black and white photos poignantly reminded the public of what happened at Gettysburg, and the nation needed a way to mourn and honor the sacrifices made on that battlefield. Recognizing this need a special dedication ceremony for the National Cemetery at Gettysburg was planned and held on November 19, 1863.

Edward Everett, a statesman and an acclaimed orator was the main speaker. He spoke for around two hours, weaving his way through history's major battles from Pericles and the Peloponnesian War to England's War of the Roses before finally getting to the Gettysburg Battle. His speech was over 13,000 words and no one remembers what he said. Then, Lincoln spoke. He famously began by saying, "Four score and seven years ago our fathers brought forth on this continent, a new nation, conceived in Liberty, and dedicated to the proposition that all men are created equal." Having stated the virtuous and noble ideals of the nation's founding, Lincoln moved onto the task at hand, dedicating this "resting place for those who here gave their lives that that nation might live." The president recognized that the suffering and sacrifices made by the men on the battlefield "have consecrated it far above our poor power to add or detract. The world will little note, nor long remember what we say here, but it can never forget what they did here." He then looked to the future saying, "...we here highly resolve that these dead shall not have died in vain – that this nation, under God, shall have a new birth of freedom, and that government of the people, by the people, for the people, shall not perish from the earth." The eloquence of Lincoln's address is unrivaled, and requires no commentary. However, wisdom from a heart in the house of mourning is subtle and easily missed. Therefore, we must take a closer look at Lincoln's words and the circumstances in which they were spoken.

Gettysburg was a great victory for the Union Army. On July 4, 1863, General Lee's Army of Northern Virginia was shattered, and on that same day, Lincoln was handed another major victory. After a long siege, the Confederate Army surrendered the town of Vicksburg, and the Union had almost complete navigational control over the Mississippi River. Only one small outpost of Confederate resistance remained on the river. After years of hardship and struggle, the war was finally turning in Lincoln's favor and a possible end was in sight. Yet, in his address there was not a hint of triumph, self-aggrandizement, or denigration of the South. Instead, he spoke of the eternal ideals of life, liberty, and equal rights, because rights come from God, not governments. Lincoln was so gracious and magnanimous that in some passages, he seems to be honoring the dead and the wounded on both sides. Not mentioning either Union or Confederate, he said, "The brave men, living and dead, who struggled here have consecrated it [the battlefield]..." Therefore, despite the hardships, suffering, and death that the South had brought to the North, Lincoln saw, not combatants but, men with souls who are created in the image of God. The president was able to resist hate, block out cries for vengeance, and speak words that are merciful, because he sensed the eternity of God that is present in Nature and man. The fragrance of heaven was the source of Lincoln's wisdom, and this eternal realm was captured in the mural that hangs above the speech.

When the architect, Henry Bacon, was designing the Lincoln Memorial, he chose a St. Louis born artist, Jules Guerin, to create two murals that depicted the principles that guided Lincoln's life. One mural hangs above the Gettysburg Address in the south chamber, and the other is above Lincoln's Second Inaugural Address in the north chamber. The murals that Guerin painted are highly allegorical, and one panel of the mural in the south chamber is particularly telling. Immortality, i.e., the Eternal, is represented by a woman, who is seated, and standing behind her chair are figures representing Faith, Hope, and Charity. In words, Lincoln painted Immortality, Faith, Hope, and Charity into the Gettysburg Address, and Guerin painted them in watercolor to hang in the president's memorial. How wonderfully fitting! Now it is time to go into the north chamber and discover more wisdom born in Lincoln's house of mourning.

Inscribed in the north wall is Lincoln's Second Inaugural Address. President Lincoln delivered this address on March 4, 1865 from the steps of the Capitol. Work to replace the old dome with a new fireproof iron dome was nearly complete and photographs show that the Capitol in 1865 looked very much as it does day. What is different from then to now, however, is where America looks for wisdom. In 1865, Americans looked to the Bible for wisdom, and Lincoln's speech that inauguration day is like a sermon complete with scripture. To fully appreciate the biblical wisdom of Lincoln's address, we must understand the events of the time. The Union army was on the cusp of total victory. The South lay in ruins. In November 1864, Atlanta came under Union Army control. General Sherman's March to the Sea was completed in December of that year, and Savannah was occupied by Union troops. Petersburg, just south of the Confederate capital of Richmond, had been under siege for months, and Richmond could fall any day. Lincoln rode these victories to reelection, and now he stood on the steps of the Capitol to take the Oath of Office for a second time. Would he tout his victories, posture triumphantly, or speak of vengeance against the rebellious South? We know from his Gettysburg Address that such vain conceits were not in his character. What came from Lincoln that March day was wisdom from above.

He began the speech by a factual recounting of how the war was going, and regarding how or when the war might end, he said, "With high hope for the future, no prediction in regard to it is ventured." He then talked about how the war started saying, "Both parties depreciated war, but one of them would make war rather than let the nation survive, and the other would accept war rather than let it perish. And war came." At this point, Lincoln had spoken for about two minutes, and over the next three minutes, as if it were a sermon, he quoted the Bible and talked of God's providence in the affairs of men and nations.

About the North and the South, he said, "Both read the same Bible and pray to the same God, and each invokes His aid against the other. It may seem strange that any men should dare to ask a just God's assistance in wringing their bread from the sweat of other men's faces, let us judge not, that we be not judged. The prayers of both could not be answered. That of neither has been answered fully. The Almighty has His own purposes." In this passage Lincoln condemned slavery, but he did it in the context of man's sinfulness before a righteous and just God. Lincoln clearly saw the South as being in the wrong, but he left judgment up to God and quoted Jesus' words from Matthew 7:1 that in the King James Version reads, *Judge not, that ye be not judged.* Next, he spoke of slavery as being an offense to God, and that this war is God's providence to remove that offense. Lincoln said, "He now wills to remove [slavery], and that He gives to both North and South this terrible war as the woe due to those by whom the offense came..." Speaking further about God's providence, Lincoln said, "Fondly do we hope, fervently do we pray, that this mighty scourge of war may speedily pass away. Yet, if God wills that it continue until all the wealth piled by the bondsman's two hundred and fifty years of unrequited toil shall be sunk, and until every drop of blood drawn with the lash shall be paid by another drawn with the sword, as was said three thousand years ago, so still it must be said, 'the judgments of the Lord are true and righteous altogether.'"

An estimated 620,000 men died fighting the Civil War, and in the 1860's that figure was about 2% of the population. Extrapolated to today's population that's roughly 6 million men dying in the line of duty, and this figure doesn't account for civilian causalities. Lincoln called it a "terrible war," and indeed it was. The world never before had witnessed this level of death and destruction, and even World War II would not surpass the Civil War in terms of American combat deaths. Lincoln's heart lived in this house of war, death, and mourning. Yet the wisdom that came from this experience is humility before God to accept the war as His judgment for the sin of African slavery. Now with the end of the war in sight, the wisdom that was born in the house of mourning moved Lincoln to speak of love, healing the nation's wounds, and peace. Lincoln concluded his address saying, "With malice toward none, with charity for all, with firmness in the right as God gives us to see the right, let us strive on to finish the work we are in, to bind up the nation's wounds, to care for him who shall have borne the battle and for his widow and his orphan, to do all which may achieve and cherish a just and lasting peace among ourselves and with all nations."

Lincoln's wise desire for a just and peaceful post-war America is symbolically captured in Guerin's mural that hangs above his Second Inaugural Address. In the center panel of the mural, Guerin painted the Angel of Truth, who is flanked by two figures representing the North and the South. The Angel of Truth takes the hand of each and joins them together. With peace established, the best of mankind can flourish. Therefore, Guerin surrounded the Angel of Truth and the figures of the North and South with characters representing the arts and sciences – Painting, Philosophy, Music, Architecture, Chemistry, Literature, and Sculpture. Eternity is painted into the mural as well.

A haggard, wretched man is shown kneeling next to the figure representing Music, and this desperate man clutches at her knees, as if he is attempting to pull her down. He represents war and death that pulls down from humanity all the joy and delight that is Music, but she remains standing, because she is sheltered by the wings of the Angel of Truth. Standing behind Music is a mysterious cloaked figure. A mask covers his mouth and nose thus hiding his identity. He represents the future that is unwritten, and what Lincoln did in his Second Inaugural Address was listen to his heart and tell how the future should be written. America's future, he said, should be one of malice toward none, charity to all, righteousness before God, compassion, and lasting peace. This is wisdom from Lincoln's heart that lived in the house of mourning.

The Second Inaugural Address took about five minutes to deliver. Seemingly with equal speed were the events in Lincoln's life after the address. A month after the inauguration, Richmond fell on Sunday, April 2. The president and his son, Tad, visited Richmond days later, and Lincoln sat at the desk used by the president of the Confederate States, Jefferson Davis. A week later on Sunday, April 9th General Lee surrendered the Army of Northern Virginia to General Grant at Appomattox Court House. Six days later, the president was assassinated, while attending a play at Ford's Theater in Washington. Lincoln once said, "In the end, it's not the years in your life that count. It's the life in your years." Those difficult years of life that he lived during his presidency were true life indeed. The wisdom he bequeathed America endures, because it came from the eternal.

After seven years of construction, the Lincoln Memorial was dedicated on May 30, 1922. President Warren G. Harding and Chief Justice of the Supreme Court, William Howard Taft, who was a former president, as well, gave speeches. Lincoln's son, the 79 year old Robert Todd Lincoln, was an honored dignitary at the dedication. Since its dedication, the Lincoln Memorial has been the site of many important events, and certainly none was more important than Dr. Martin Luther King's "I Have a Dream" speech. An estimated quarter of a million people were on the National Mall to hear Dr. King's words that were delivered on August 28, 1963. It was a high point in America's Civil Rights Movement, and "I Have a Dream" rightfully belongs among one of the most important speeches in American history. It was eloquently written and spoken with righteous passion, but perhaps what makes Dr. King's speech so enduring is the wisdom in it that came from the same source as Lincoln's wisdom. It came from a heart in the house of mourning. Sadly, Dr. King's life, like that of President Lincoln, was cut short by assassination.

One hundred and sixty years have passed since Lincoln's Gettysburg Address, and it was 60 years ago that Dr. King stood on the steps of the Lincoln Memorial and gave his "I Have a Dream" speech. Certainly in the ensuing years, America has seen a few wise leaders come and go, but none of the stature of Lincoln or King. Why? In more than a century and a half, a nation as large, populous, and free as America should surely have at least one or two additional towering figures of wisdom, but we don't. Again, why? Perhaps, the National Mall holds the answer.

A nation's memorials are windows into the soul of the people for the memorials tell what the people value, honor, and hold sacred. Since the Lincoln Memorial was dedicated in 1922, several memorials have been added. All, except one, the Martin Luther King Memorial, are war memorials. World War II, the Korean War, and the Vietnam War are all memorialized, and the wartime president, Franklin Delano Roosevelt, is honored with a memorial. However, the FDR Memorial is different from previous presidential memorials, and it's even different from the MLK Memorial. FDR is honored, not for wisdom, but for his leadership achievements during the Great Depression and World War II. The other memorials to Washington, Jefferson, Lincoln, and King honor the men and the wisdom of their ideals.

From the mid- 20th Century to the 21st Century, with the exception of Martin Luther King, America has, on the National Mall, honored no man or woman of conscience, wisdom, and ideals. Yet we have multiple memorials to wars. This is not to say that those who sacrificed in those wars should not be honored. Rather it is to ask what are the ideals for which they made their great sacrifice? Ideals must be articulated and renewed by each generation. More importantly, they must be internalized and applied to the challenges and issues of the day. Such application requires men and women, who can see with the eyes of the heart and with the eyes of the mind. They are the wise. They are the ones that America needs today.

Our visit to the Lincoln Memorial is now complete. In the central chamber, we take one last look at America's 16th president, and take a moment to read the inscription on the wall behind his statue. It reads:

IN THIS TEMPLE AS IN THE HEARTS OF THE PEOPLE
FOR WHOM HE SAVED THE UNION THE MEMORY OF
ABRAHAM LINCOLN IS ENSHRINED FOREVER

Before leaving Lincoln's temple, we must make sure that we are enshrining forever the complete man. In his two most famous addresses, we have seen wisdom from a man whose heart was in the house of mourning. However, does this mean that a wise person is perpetually sad and somber? No! By all accounts, Lincoln had a wonderful sense of humor. He was a backwoodsman, who enjoyed spinning a yarn and laughing, even about something as important as the Emancipation Proclamation.

After reading an early draft of the Emancipation Proclamation, Lincoln gathered his cabinet to discuss the document and he began the discussion by reading a humorous story. Some members of his cabinet told him it was inappropriate to be telling jokes before discussing something so serious. Lincoln reportedly replied, "Gentlemen, why don't you laugh? With the fearful strain that is upon me night and day, if I did not laugh I should die, and you need this medicine as much as I do." Lincoln loved to laugh. We cannot and should not be perpetually sad or perpetually seeking the next fun thing. That's not the way God made us. He made us in His image and that image includes joy, laughter, and fun. God also gave us a life, where no one escapes loss, sadness, or defeat. Therefore, we all have spent or one day will spend time in the house of mourning. If while we are there we sense the presence of God, who dwells in eternity, the experience makes us wiser, and it grants something else – joy and an even deeper appreciation of life. Therefore, joy, laughter, and fun are part of wisdom too. We see it in Lincoln and it is why he is honored in this temple. Indeed, *the heart of the wise is in the house of mourning.*

Chapter 13.
RESOLVE... to find God's path
and remain on it.

After leaving Sukkoth they camped at Etham on the edge of the desert. [21] By day the Lord went ahead of them in a pillar of cloud to guide them on their way and by night in a pillar of fire to give them light, so that they could travel by day or night. [22] Neither the pillar of cloud by day nor the pillar of fire by night left its place in front of the people. (Exodus 13:20-22)

How exhilarating it must have been that night camped on the edge of the desert! And, how frightening and dreadful it must have been too. Only a day or so earlier, the Children of Israel with Moses leading them, started their trek out of Egypt. Slaves, who were now loaded with possessions, gathered as families and tribes and walked out of the greatest and most powerful nation in the ancient world. Shockingly, the possessions they carried were given to them by their Egyptian masters, who were panicked. Everyone in Egypt – both slaves and masters – had witnessed the miracles that God had performed through Moses and Aaron. The final miracle, the Passover, that took the lives of Egypt's firstborn sons, while sparing or passing over, the firstborn sons of the Children of Israel broke the Egyptians' will.

Pharaoh told Moses and Aaron, *"Up! Leave my people, you and the Israelites! Go, worship the Lord as you have requested. Take your flocks and herds, as you have said, and go. And also bless me."* (Exodus 12:31-32) The Exodus was now underway, but before they left, Moses told the Israelites to ask the Egyptians for silver, gold, and clothing. The Book of Exodus records, *they gave them what they asked for; so they plundered the Egyptians.* (12:36) Then, they were off, step-by-step walking away from the land that had been their home for 430 years. Now, this mass of tribal people was camped on the edge of the desert at Etham.

As the sun set, what a sight it must have been! Glowing softly in the gathering darkness, hundreds of campfires dotted the landscape. Twilight had not yet given way to darkness, and the *pillar of cloud* that had guided them throughout the day was stationary and visible. The *pillar of fire to give them light* at night would soon arrive. In this moment as day slipped into night, the brightest early evening stars began to out shine the waning sun. Soon, the nighttime desert sky would be lit with millions of stars. The mighty hand of Almighty God had brought them out of Egypt, and his Presence was among them in the cloud by day and the fire by night. What could be more comforting and reassuring than knowing that Yahweh, the God of the Promise was with them? Yet beyond God's light in the camp stood a dark and forbidding desert.

The Children of Israel could only guess about what was in front of them or behind them. Was Pharaoh's army on the march? They knew him to be ruthless and determined. Was he really going to let his slaves just walk away? And what of their former masters? The reality that their silver and gold were gone must have them seething with anger. Surely trouble was brewing behind them, and what was in front of them on this night? A dry and barren land of searing heat by day, freezing nights, and home to scorpions, serpents, and a host of creatures they would soon call "unclean." Their lives had been spent in the Nile River valley that was lush, green, and verdant. They weren't equipped to live in the desert and yet that's where Moses was leading them!

The exhilarating, energizing part of the Exodus was over. Saying "Adios!" and making a dramatic exit was done. Anyone trapped in a dismal job dreams of that day, and the Children of Israel got it. Now, the hard part was here. They had to cross a desert, and they knew that whatever was out there in the night beyond their camp at Etham, they would have to face it in the morning. Fears, doubts, and reservations had to be put aside, and resolutions made to put one foot in front of the other and walk into the desert. But, they weren't alone. The Lord God was with them, and despite all their grumbling and complaining to Moses and Aaron, every day for 40 years they walked toward the Promised Land. This is resolve and for the Children of Israel, the vision was freedom in a land of their own, but that was not what kept them going for so long. Their resolve came from faith that God was true to his Word. When they doubted, their resolve vanished and they wandered. Then, God raised up a new generation, who believed his Word, and shared the resolve to accomplish the vision and enter the Promised Land.

In America today, resolve is limited solely to individual pursuits aimed at benefiting or enriching oneself. Americans celebrate individuals, who resolve to become the best professional athlete, the greatest performing artist, the most famous actor, or the richest person in the world. But, what do Americas believe today and what do we as a people jointly resolve to accomplish? Not that long ago, it was putting a man on the moon and returning him safely. Before that feat, it was winning World War II. A century earlier, it was creating a free and prosperous nation that stretched from the Atlantic to the Pacific, and before that is was ending the moral stain of slavery at the cost of 600,000 American lives in the Civil War. Such was America's resolve! Yet what of today? Could it be that this current generation of Americans is unlike previous generations? Is the reason Americans are wandering, aimless, and so lacking in a shared resolve the same reason that caused a generation of ancient Israelites to wander? That reason being a disbelief in God's Word.

Wandering vs. resolve. Does it really come down to a choice of whether we believe God's Word or not? Let's meet a man who will tell us. In the 19th Century, he was an internationally recognized scientist, whose discoveries were immensely beneficial to the world. He was at the height of his scientific career when Charles Darwin in 1859 published "On the Origin of the Species" that disputed God's Word in Genesis. Yet in this climate of newly blossoming doubt and open rejection of God's Word, this man never doubted. He believed that every aspect and detail of God's Word were true and applicable to every arena of life, including science. In fact, his scientific publications quoted scripture. Because he believed God's Word, he resolved to know what was considered unknowable, and to find what everyone from the dawn of human history thought unfindable. Then, when he discovered it, he freely shared it with the world. Wealth or fame were never his motivation. Right now, he's on a special mission aboard a ship. Let's join him on the deck.

* * *

Aboard the *USS Brandywine* off the coast of Cape Henry, Virginia, where the Chesapeake meets the Atlantic, September 8, 1825.

> *The wind blows to the south*
> *and turns to the north;*
> *round and round it goes,*
> *ever returning on its course.*
> *All streams flow into the sea,*
> *yet the sea is never full.*
> *To the place the streams come from,*
> *there they return again.* (Ecclesiastes 1:6-7)

As the *Brandywine's* sails filled with a south wind, 19 year-old Midshipman Matthew Fontaine Maury recalled these verses written by King Solomon thousands of years ago. The Bible he knew, the sea he did not. His father, Richard, was a devout Huguenot Protestant, and his grandfather, the Reverend James

Maury, was a Christian scholar and teacher, who taught Thomas Jefferson, as a boy. The Bible tells us that as the twig is bent so grows the tree, and in the Maury family, the Bible was read every day, shaping Matthew who could quote lengthy passages from memory. Recalling this passage from Ecclesiastes was not a problem. The Bible he knew, and the sea? This day was the first time he had seen the ocean from the deck of a ship, and he stood in the bow transfixed, staring at the endless water before him.

The Maury's were an old and distinguished Virginia family, and Matthew was born in Spotsylvania County, Virginia. However, he grew up in Franklin, Tennessee, far from the sea. He was a farm boy, but farming never suited him, and when Sam Houston, a family friend and Tennessee's representative in Congress, secured a midshipman's appointment for him, Maury took it. Now, he was here aboard the *Brandywine*, a brand new three-masted, 44-gun frigate. Suddenly, the ship pitched and groaned under the strain of a fresh wind and the swells of open water. They were in the Atlantic. Ensign Maury clutched the railing and turned to watch the coast of Virginia recede behind him. As he steadied himself on the rolling deck, he spotted Captain Charles Morris talking with the *Brandywine's* distinguished guest passenger and the reason for this voyage. The Marquis de Lafayette, the famous Revolutionary War general and close personal friend of George Washington, had completed his grand and celebrated tour of the United States and was returning home to France. In fact, the *Brandywine* had been commissioned and built in Washington, D.C.'s Navy Yard just for the purpose of transporting General Lafayette.

Lafayette caught Maury's stare and tipped his hat. Captain Morris then spotted him, and shouted, "Look lively Mr. Maury." Matthew Fontaine Maury was now in the United States Navy and now at sea. The Bible he knew, the sea he did not. At that moment, he could have never imagined that, because he knew the

Bible, he would soon so thoroughly know the sea that he would be called the "Pathfinder of the Seas."

Brandywine's voyage to France was difficult. The ship leaked, the weather was, as General Lafayette said, "Tres mal temps," and much to the disappointment of the officers, the aging Lafayette, suffering from seasickness, spent most of the Atlantic crossing in his cabin. But this was navy life and Maury took to it with the zeal, enthusiasm, and unrivaled resolve that would characterize his entire career. His attention to detail, keen mind, and insightful observations caught the attention of his superiors.

Maury spent much of the next nine years at sea, and four of those years were aboard the *USS Vincennes*, a 127-foot Boston-class sloop. The *Vincennes* set sail from New York in September 1826 and returned in June 1830. It was the first U.S. naval vessel to circumnavigate the globe. After so much time at sea, the crew was granted extended leave and during this time, Maury fell deeply in love with his cousin, Ann Herndon of Fredericksburg, Virginia. Eventually, even the longest shore leave must end, and he was assigned to a new ship, the *Falmouth.* He and Ann vowed to write often and he gave her a special imprint for sealing the wax on her letters to him. The seal was a one-word inscription: *Mizpah*, which in Hebrew means "The Lord watch between thee and me when are absent one from the other."

In July 1834, Matthew and Ann married, and settled into life in Fredericksburg, where they began a family. Maury remained in the navy, was promoted to lieutenant, and during this period ashore, he published his first scientific article, entitled "On the Navigation of Cape Horn." A book would soon follow. In 1836, "A New Theoretical and Practical Treatise on Navigation" became a landmark naval publication. Lt. Maury's reputation grew, but in 1839 it appeared that his career as a naval officer might well be over.

In the summer of 1839, he was surveying U.S. ports in the Gulf of Mexico, when new orders arrived. He was to report to New York Harbor, where he would join the crew of the *Consort.* Maury decided to make this long journey overland. After visiting his family in Tennessee, he made his way to Ohio and boarded a stagecoach that was headed East. Near Somerset, Ohio at one o'clock in the morning during a storm, the rain-swollen road collapsed under the stagecoach wheels, sending the coach, horses, and passengers tumbling down an embankment. Maury was thrown from the coach and suffered a severe leg injury, breaking his right knee and fracturing his femur. For months, he was unable to leave Somerset, and when he finally returned home to Fredericksburg, he learned that the leg had been improperly set. Without anesthesia – which was not yet discovered – Maury's leg was broken again and set correctly. Once healed, Maury's seaworthiness was questioned, and while he applied for ship board duty, he failed to receive any postings. On July 1, 1842, he finally was assigned as the officer in charge of the Depot of Charts and Instruments in Washington, D.C.

The Depot was basically a storage room for ships' logs, maps, charts, tables of tides, wind speeds and direction, and every sort of maritime data. Imagine at 36 years of age with ambitions to advance in rank, you are pigeon-holed in a storage room filled with disorganized stacks and stacks of papers. For most men, it signals that their career is over. Put in an appearance, make the minimal effort, take long lunches, and collect a paycheck, but Maury was not most men. He dove into the task at hand. He developed a methodology to catalog and organize all the information, and then he poured over the data. With only pen and paper – no computer spreadsheets – he identified and recorded relationships within this vast amount of data. He produced new worldwide nautical maps, showing currents, prevailing wind speed and direction. His first publication of "Wind and Current

Charts" appeared in 1847 and it was updated periodically as he developed new information.

In this era of sailing ships' Maury's publications were invaluable to shipping companies, navies, and anyone who ventured on the high seas. Building upon this success, Maury devised an international standardized methodology for collecting and recording maritime data that was adopted by nations around the world. He arranged for the newly collected data to be sent to him in Washington, D.C., thus creating a global repository for oceanic information.

Under Maury's leadership, the Depot was no longer a dusty forgotten closet where careers ended. Aspiring young officers requested assignment, and under President John Quincy Adams, the Depot became part of the Naval Observatory. Single-handedly, Maury created oceanography, meteorology, and physical geography. He identified the Gulf Stream and improved navigation worldwide. He observed the migrating pattern of whales, and proposed that under the Arctic ice was a sea that connected the Atlantic to the Pacific Ocean. He studied the formation of coral islands and the movement of nutrients in the ocean. He mapped the bottom of the Atlantic and was an advisor for the project to submerge the first transatlantic telegraph cable running from Nova Scotia to Ireland. His book, *The Physical Geography of the Sea,* was hailed as a monumental achievement. His fame was worldwide. He lectured throughout Europe, and received numerous awards, including a series of silver medals commissioned by Pope Pius IX.

How many millennia has man sailed the oceans? Four? Perhaps longer? And in those thousands of years, the sea remained an enigma, the source of myth, the domain of monsters and mermaids, and a fickle mistress, who one day is calm and serene and the next will take the life of any mariner foolish enough to venture upon her waters. Throughout these thousands of years, man assembled only the crudest and rudimentary information about the oceans. Tides could be predicted and the prevailing winds for each season foretold, and that was it! It wasn't until 1492, that man, i.e., Columbus, decided to sail as far out into the Atlantic as he could. Then in the 19th Century over a period of less than four decades, Matthew Fontaine Maury added more knowledge and information about the world's oceans than had been learned over the preceding four thousand years. Why? How?

At a young age, he resolved to believe God's Word. Daily, his family read the Bible and in particular Psalms, which tells of *the paths of the seas*. Passages from Psalms 8 and 107 caught the attention of young Maury.

You have made them [human beings] *a little lower than the angels*
and crowned them with glory and honor.
⁶ *You made them rulers over the works of your hands;*
you put everything under their feet:
⁷ *all flocks and herds,*
and the animals of the wild,
⁸ *the birds in the sky,*
and the fish in the sea,
all that swim the paths of the seas.
⁹ *Lord, our Lord,*
how majestic is your name in all the earth!
(Psalm 8:5-9)

Psalm 107 speaks of *wonderful deeds in the deep.*
Some went out on the sea in ships;
they were merchants on the mighty waters.
²⁴ *They saw the works of the Lord,*
his wonderful deeds in the deep. (Psalm 107:23-24)

Because Maury believed that God's Word is true, he resolved to find the *paths of the seas* where the fish swim, and he vowed to explore God's *wonderful deeds in the deep.* Joshua led the Children of Israel into the Promised Land by faith in God's Word, and Maury led the world into a "Promised Land," of safer and more efficient ocean travel, based on the same faith. In 1849, it took 180 days to sail from New York around Cape Horn and on to San Francisco. Due to Maury's discoveries, the trip was reduced by 47 days, and similar efficiencies were made for ships sailing from England to Australia. He made these discoveries because where other men saw only random chaos in the oceans, Maury saw a divine plan written in scripture and he resolved to find it.

On October 10, 1860, Maury was the keynote speaker to dedicate the laying of the cornerstone for the University of the South at Sewanee, Tennessee. The University of the South was founded by southern dioceses of the Episcopal Church. When the cornerstone was laid that October day in 1860, eight bishops, 200 elders, and five thousand people were in attendance. Maury spoke at length and was interrupted numerous times with applause. His speech was an epic chronicling of 19th Century physical geography and earth science. Concerning the source of his inspiration and resolve, he said:

"I have been blamed by men of science, both in this country and in England, for quoting the Bible in confirmation of the doctrines of physical geography. The Bible, they say, was not written for scientific purposes, and is therefore of no authority in matters of science. I beg pardon! The Bible *is* authority for everything it touches. What would you think of the historian who should refuse to consult the historical records of the Bible, because the Bible was not written for the purposes of history? The Bible is true and science is true. The agents [meaning the forces of nature] concerned in the physical economy of our planet are ministers of His who made both it and the Bible. The records which He has chosen to make through the agency of these ministers of His upon the crust of the earth are as true as the records which, by the hands of His prophets and servants, He has been pleased to make in the Book of Life. They are both true; and when your men of science, with vain and hasty conceit, announce the discovery of disagreement between them, rely upon it the fault is not with the Witness or His records, but the 'worm' who essays to interpret evidence which he does not understand." Toward the end of his speech, Maury said, "Thus as we progress with our science we are permitted now and then to point out here and there in the physical machinery of the earth a design of the Great Architect, when He planned it all."

When the Children of Israel believed the promises in God's Word, they accomplished the seemingly impossible – from slavery to a great nation. Likewise, Maury, who believed God's Word, accomplished the seemingly impossible – he found the paths of the seas, and is forever known as the "Pathfinder of the Seas." This is a lovely and fitting end to Maury's story. Unfortunately, it is not the end. There is another chapter in Maury's life to be told, and it is of wandering; losing his way like the Children of Israel.

Roughly, six months after his 1860 speech at the University of the South, Maury's life – and the United States – was turned upside down. Maury was no great supporter of African slavery in the South, but his opposition to it seemed to be more practical than moral. As a result, his views on slavery were inconsistent with Christ's command to love one another. On this matter, he was sadly a product of his time, as were most people in the South, including pastors, elders, and parishioners. With Lincoln's inauguration, Southern states began succeeding from the Union, and battle lines were being drawn. By citizenship, Maury was a Tennessean and by birth and legacy, he was a Virginian. When both states succeeded, Maury resigned his commission as a Commander in the U.S. Navy to become Commander in the

Confederate States Navy and head of its Naval Bureau of Coast, Harbor, and River Defense. In this role, Maury did not engage in direct naval warfare, but he did design a lethal "torpedo mine" that was highly effective against Union warships. However, the majority of the Civil War, Maury was in England securing and equipping ships for use in the Confederate Navy. At the conclusion of the war in 1865, Maury, fearing arrest, did not immediately return home to Virginia. Instead, he remained in Europe and engaged in a scheme with Archduke Maximilian of Austria to establish a colony in Mexico for former Confederates. The idea was eventually abandoned and he returned home in 1868.

It is ironic that a man, who resolved to believe God's Word so literally that it guided his research, could at the same time ignore Christ's great command to love one another. Yet it is so very human too, and during those Civil War years and in the immediate aftermath, Maury's life wandered off course just like the Children of Israel in the desert, who did not believe all of God's Word. From Maury's life story and the story of the Children of Israel, the message is clear. If we are to enter whatever "Promised Land" God has destined for us, we must resolve to find and stay on the path that God has prescribed in the Bible. Yet, when our resolve fails and we wander, the Lord God, who knows us and loves us, forgives us. Maury's life teaches us this aspect of scripture of too.

After returning to Virginia in 1868, Maury took a faculty position at the Virginia Military Institute in Lexington. He resumed his research, and with the seemingly limitless energy and enthusiasm that characterized all his endeavors, he lectured, traveled, and wrote. But in 1873, his energy waned, and he became ill on a lecture tour. He returned home to Lexington as quickly as possible, and when he entered the house, he said to his wife, "My dear, I am come home to die," and he went immediately to bed. The family gathered and his condition worsened.

Thirty years earlier, when he was alone in Ohio recuperating from the stagecoach accident that mangled his knee and broke his leg, he wrote a prayer. Each day for 30 years, he prayed this prayer and in his life-long prayer we see Maury's heart. Now on his death bed, he prayed it a final time. He said, "Lord Jesus, thou Son of God and Redeemer of the world, have mercy upon me! Pardon my offenses, and teach me the error of my ways; give me a new heart and a right mind. Teach me and all mine to do Thy will, and in all things to keep Thy law. Teach me also to ask those things necessary for eternal life. Lord, pardon me for all my sins, for Thine is the kingdom and the power and the glory, forever and ever. Amen."

Matthew Fontaine Maury knew the Bible, and because he knew the Bible, he and the world came to know the sea.

> *[T]he fish in the sea,*
> *all that swim the paths of the seas.*
> *⁹ Lord, our Lord,*
> *how majestic is your name in all the earth!*
> (Psalm 8:5-9)

This is a poignant and fitting end to Maury's story, but it's not the end. There is more to his life's story that tells of wandering vs. resolve, and finding – or not – God's path in life.

After Maury's death on February 1, 1873, newspapers in America and Europe carried numerous eulogies, and barely was the ink dry on these tributes before the floodgates of honors opened. The United States Naval Academy named a hall in his honor, as did the Virginia Military Institute. The Maury River in Virginia bears his name, as does a lake, numerous elementary and high schools, and various U.S. ships. In the 1920's, decades after his death, money was raised to place a memorial to Commander Maury on Monument Avenue in Richmond, Virginia. Impressive statues to other sons of Virginia – JEB Stuart, Robert E. Lee, Jefferson Davis, and Stonewall Jackson – were already positioned on the grassy boulevard. These were the leaders and heroes of the Confederacy yet Maury's place among them was not due to his role in the Civil War. He spent most of the war in England, and the Confederate Navy had some victories, but never seriously challenged the supremacy of the U.S. Navy. His place on Monument Avenue was not merited by his Civil War activities, but because of his scientific accomplishments. His memorial artistically reflected this fact.

Maury's bronze and white marble memorial was massive, and at the time of its dedication in 1929, everyone agreed that the sculptor, F. William Sievers, had captured the essence of the man. Maury, cast in bronze, was seated. His right hand held a pencil and compass, and in his left was a chart, as if he was calculating the navigation of an unseen ship, and instructing the captain on the course to set. Behind his chair rose a white marble column, whose mass seemed large and sturdy enough to support the world, and indeed it did for at the top of the column sat a bronze globe depicting Earth's great oceans. Set upon the oceans in bronze relief was a school of fish swimming a path known only to the fish, God, and Maury. Then, in the smallest of details, a feature so easily missed, Sievers revealed the heart of Maury. Lying next to Maury's chair was the Bible. Sievers truly created a masterpiece of public art that was paid for in part by money collected from schoolchildren across the Commonwealth of Virginia. Sadly, the monument is no more.

For nearly one hundred years, Maury's memorial stood on Monument Avenue as a witness to a man of faith and science, who resolved to follow what he knew to be true. Then, in the summer of 2020 riots erupted across America, including Richmond. Statues and monuments with any association to African slavery or the Civil War were targeted for destruction.

Even Washington, Jefferson, Lincoln, and Columbus were not safe from mobs intent on erasing all that previous generations of Americans had held to be good, honorable, and worthy of memorializing. On July 2, 2020, Richmond's mayor declared Maury's memorial a threat to public safety and it was removed and destroyed. Yet, within this mindlessly vindictive destruction is Maury's final lesson for us. Civilizations that resolve to follow their own paths rather than God's never enter the Promised Land. In their arrogance, they are destined to failure and destruction unless they change course.

The generation of Children of Israel, who abandoned God, never entered the Promised Land. It was the faith and resolve of their children that built a great nation. Perhaps, it will be so with America. If it pleases God, a new generation of Americans, who possess Maury's resolve in both faith and science, will arise to lead America into a new era of freedom, peace, and achievement. This journey to the future begins by daily resolving to find God's path and remain on it.

Source: Charles Lee Lewis, <u>Matthew Fontaine Maury, the Pathfinder of the Seas</u>, published by Good Press, 2022, but written ca. 1925.

Chapter 14.
VIRTUE... found and America's new dawn

Our journey to discover the virtues that made America began in Chapter 1 with the story of Major Charles Davis in Bath, England. In 1873, he was the city's surveyor and architect, who was assigned the task of locating the source of a leak that was draining the King's Bath. Underneath the pool, he found the leak and in the process discovered the true foundation that supported the City of Bath. It was the substantial walls and massive columns built by the Romans centuries earlier. The Roman structures endured because the builders were constructing a bath and temple complex to one of their many gods, Sulis Minerva, a local deity that merged the traits of a Celtic god, Sulis, with the Greco-Roman god, Minerva. To rightly honor a god, a Roman temple had to be substantial, enduring, dignified, and handsomely decorated, and in honoring the god, the citizens of Bath were honoring themselves. Their god was worthy of a magnificent temple, because they themselves were worthy. The temple and baths testified to all who entered what the people of Bath believed about the gods, themselves, and the world around them.

In the 5th Century, the Romans left Britain, the island was Christianized, the Roman gods were forgotten, and the City of Bath over the centuries used the Roman foundation to build new and different structures. The ancient foundation supported all that was built and piled on top of it, as the modern City of Bath grew and developed. Gradually, all that the Romans had built disappeared from sight beneath the streets of Bath. For centuries, the Roman foundation slept and waited to be rediscovered. When Major Davis reported his discovery, the City of Bath determined that such enduring and ancient beauty underneath their city should be preserved and revealed so that the world may know what made Bath the city that it is. Structures covering the temple and bath complex were demolished and removed, and with care, walls and artifacts were cleaned, repaired, and displayed for all to see. Today, thousands of visitors tour Bath's Roman foundation.

Rome, of course, never founded a colony in America, and it would be roughly a thousand years after the fall of Rome that Christopher Columbus sailed to the New World. Yet America has a foundation that is older, more enduring, more substantial, more massive, more beautiful, more dignified, and more impressive than what the Romans constructed in Bath for their god, Sulis Minerva. America's foundation is spiritual, and make no mistake, when the Roman's built the temple and bath complex it was a spiritual place that served a civic function. So it is with America. From its religious and spiritual foundation came the civics that resulted in the United States.

Just as Bath built over its Roman foundation, America has built over the nation's spiritual foundation. The virtuous pillars of Judeo-Christianity that support the United States government, America's institutions, and the American way of life are today hidden under a godless, virtueless faux foundation that is cracking and springing leaks just like the foundation under the King's Bath. Meanwhile, the virtuous spiritual foundation that led to America's greatness lies silent under Americans' feet just as the great Roman foundation slept under the streets of Bath. When the citizens of Bath discovered what was lost and forgotten, they embraced it, restored it, announced it to the world, and experienced a revival. The question is what will America do?

Through the pages of this book, we have been like Major Davis, who with torch in hand, made his initial exploration of the magnificent foundation of Bath. He didn't see and find everything on that first trip, and neither have we discovered all the beauty of America's spiritual foundation. Yet, we've made a start. We've completed our initial exploration and seen the steady and enduring Christian virtues that made America. What shall we do with this information?

After his discovery, Major Davis had no grand plan. He simply told people what he had found and gradually the citizens of Bath understood what they had lost and charted a course to recover it. But, Bath didn't change overnight. It took decades before the Roman foundation was completely uncovered, and it may well be decades before America uncovers and returns to our spiritual foundation. However, at least we now have an idea of what we've lost, and we need to begin removing everything that hides our true spiritual foundation. Bath had to demolish and remove buildings that hid the Roman foundation, and America's revival requires demolition too, but not the physical kind. America's revival will begin when the lies that obscure and hide America's Christian foundation are bulldozed and deposited into the dustbin of history. This demolition will take time. Therefore, we must be patient and while anticipating America's revival, we must live virtuous lives.

Living a virtuous life is not a self-improvement project. In fact, it's quite the opposite. Self-improvement means waking up in the morning and vowing to live more courageously, or more wisely, or to be more forgiving, or more of any of the other virtues. While laudable, it doesn't work. The virtues are not stand alone behavioral characteristics. The humble person is also the person who is naturally civil. The person who forgives the most undoubtedly loves the most. A wise person is very likely a just person, and the hopeful person certainly has more resolve than others. Therefore, a virtuous person's life may be characterized by one or more of the virtues being more strongly represented than others, but make no mistake, all the virtues will be present to some degree in their character. Therefore, living a virtuous life is not about improving the character we already have, but changing our character all together. Such a radical change is beyond the reach of self-improvement. We need something outside of ourselves if we are to change our character.

What we need is the knowledge of God, and more specifically, the knowledge of the holiness of God. Holy means set apart and sacred. With knowledge of the holiness of God comes the understanding that since we are created in His image, we too are set apart and that human life is sacred. C.S. Lewis in a famous sermon preached in the Church of St. Mary the Virgin at Oxford College in 1942 said, "There are no ordinary people. You have never talked to a mere mortal. Nations, cultures, arts, civilizations - these are mortal, and their life is to ours as the life of a gnat. But it is immortals whom we joke with, work with, marry, snub and exploit - immortal horrors or everlasting splendors. This does not mean that we are to be perpetually solemn. We must play. But our merriment must be of that kind (and it is, in fact, the merriest kind) which exists between people who have, from the outset, taken each other seriously - no flippancy, no superiority, no presumption." The knowledge of the holiness of God coupled with the understanding that we are ourselves created in his image transforms our character. It allows the virtues to be added to our lives like adding books to a shelf. Who is handing us the virtues? It is God, because human virtues are the divine attributes of God incorporated into our character. In other words, human virtue comes from what God Himself is like.

A.W. Tozer, a 20th Century American pastor and theologian, wrote a wonderful book entitled, "The Knowledge of the Holy." In an early chapter, he defines the attributes of God as "whatever God has in any way revealed as being true of himself." (p. 12) Tozer then describes the attributes of God as being wisdom, justice, goodness, grace, faithfulness, mercifulness, and love.

Our lives are virtuous, when we know and love God, and desire to live into his godly attributes. This side of heaven, no one is perfect at incorporating all of God's attributes into our lives so that we are wholly virtuous. We are always works in progress, and Christian theology even has a word for our progress: sanctification. When we sanctify ourselves to Christ, He begins to weave His attributes into our character, and the effect is a steady change into a more virtuous person. Virtuous people have a profound influence, changing lives and shaping society. We've seen this influence in the stories told in the preceding chapters.

The HUMILITY of John Winthrop and the Puritans defined New England and enriched America. Winthrop's sermon on Christian humility with the line "we shall be a city upon hill" inspired Presidents Kennedy and Reagan. One man's sermon on humility guided America for generations.

The FAITH of Moravian Brethren in an Atlantic storm that threatened to sink their small wooden ship convicted a young pastor named, John Wesley, that while he had ample religion, he lacked faith. When Wesley got faith, he changed the world in the First Great Awakening, and it all began with a simple act of faith by a few people aboard a ship in the Atlantic Ocean.

In the Kentucky wilderness, a few pastors, elders, and dedicated parishioners saw hopelessness in the faces of their neighbors and through camp meetings, they brought HOPE that changed lives and started the Second Great Awakening. That same hope lives today in people touched and changed by the multiple revivals that began at Asbury University. The hope of generations started with a dozen or so people, who in 1800 practiced the virtue of hope in a wilderness.

Our Founders believed that America was a new Jerusalem, and that God's love was active in guiding the nation's affairs. They knew the virtue of LOVE, and gave us a constitutional republic for a moral people, who love God.

Jerry M. Roper, Ph.D.

That men who fought and tried to kill another could embrace each other as friends and brothers demonstrates the power of FORGIVENESS. On the 50th anniversary of the Battle of Gettysburg, veterans from the North and South met on the bloodiest part of the battlefield, where they shook hands and wished their former enemies God's peace. Forgiveness, this is America at its finest!

With COURAGE, Patrick Henry accepted that there could be no peace with King George III, and with courage, he cried "Give me liberty or give me death." Americans heard his cry and won our freedom. Just one man's courage emboldened a nation!

In the darkest hour of the Revolutionary War, George Washington demonstrated remarkable HONOR. When the general mistakenly opened a letter addressed to Joseph Reed a subordinate officer, he discovered that Reed had betrayed him by currying favor with a rival American general. Washington, because he had wrongly opened the letter, resealed it, and wrote a note of apology to Reed for mistakenly opening his mail. In practicing the virtue of honor, Washington avoided division in the army and went on to win a great victory at Trenton.

To learn of the virtue of JUSTICE, we visited a Parisian cemetery, whose most famous occupant is connected to both the American and French Revolutions. He is the Marquis de Lafayette. The injustice of France's Reign of Terror contrasts sharply with the justice of the revolution in America, and the reason for the difference is that America never forgot that justice is an attribute of God. France rejected God and his justice, while America embraced it.

The virtue of CIVILITY is the lubricant that reduces friction in society. In Colonial America, good manners and proper conduct were expected and part of society much as rudeness and disrespect are expected parts of society today. As a boy, George Washington wrote 110 axioms on proper conduct and good behavior in society. Manners, self-control, and graciousness are seemingly small things. Yet these small things shaped Washington's character as a man, a general, and president. Washington's character set the tone for governance in the fledging United States. Therefore, the small virtue of civility can make a big difference. Washington's 110 axioms are still in print and available as a small book with a big impact.

GRATITUDE – it makes the heart well. Sarah Hale had every reason to be ungrateful. Death took her beloved husband at a young age and she was left alone to support and raise five children. But, she had a gracious heart and because of her unflagging effort over decades, Thanksgiving is a national holiday. Such is the power of one grateful person!

The Lincoln Memorial on the Washington, D.C. Mall is a temple to President Lincoln's WISDOM. His Gettysburg Address and Second Inaugural Speech are chiseled into the memorial's wall. Lincoln's godly wisdom inspires and guides Americans to this day.

Because Matthew Fontaine Maury believed God's word that *the fish in the sea...swim the paths of the seas* (Psalm 8:8), he resolved to find that path. Through his remarkable RESOLVE, he found it, and in the process he changed ocean travel, and established physical geography, oceanography and meteorology as scientific disciplines. All of this happened because he believed God and practiced the virtue of resolve.

In each of these stories, we have met people, who struggled, who suffered loss, betrayal, and setbacks, and who were not perfect people. Yet, they accomplished remarkable achievements that made America. While their stories are diverse and spread across centuries, they all hold two things in common. First, they believed and trusted God, and second, they practiced virtue. It is a powerful combination! We are one nation under God, because we were a nation of virtuous men and women, and only a few of their remarkable stories have been told here. Yet through the telling of these stories it is hoped that a new generation of Americans will be inspired to live virtuous lives. We only need to trust God, and follow the last words of Patrick Henry, who in his 1799 Last Will and Testament wrote:

Reader! whoever thou art, remember this, and in thy Sphere, practice Virtue thyself, and encourage it in others."